BAD JOBS and POOR DECISIONS

BAD JOBS and POOR DECISIONS

Dispatches from the Working Class

J. R. HELTON

a memoir

Liveright Publishing Corporation

A Division of W. W. Norton & Company
Independent Publishers Since 1923
New York   London

Copyright © 2018 by J. R. Helton

All rights reserved
Printed in the United States of America
First Edition

For information about permission to reproduce selections from this book, write to Permissions, Liveright Publishing Corporation, a division of W. W. Norton & Company, Inc., 500 Fifth Avenue, New York, NY 10110

For information about special discounts for bulk purchases, please contact W. W. Norton Special Sales at specialsales@wwnorton.com or 800-233-4830

Manufacturing by LSC Communications Harrisonburg
Book design by Lovedog Studio
Production manager: Lauren Abbate

Library of Congress Cataloging-in-Publication Data

Names: Helton, J. R. (John R.), author.
Title: Bad jobs and poor decisions : dispatches from the working class /
    J.R. Helton.
Other titles: Dispatches from the working class
Description: First edition. | New York : Liveright Publishing Corporation, a
    division of W. W. Norton & Company, [2018]
Identifiers: LCCN 2017032065 | ISBN 9781631492877 (hardcover)
Subjects: LCSH: Helton, J. R. (John R.) | Working class men—Texas—
    Biography. | Man-woman relationships—Texas. | Texas—Social life and
    customs—20th century. | Working class—United States—Social
    conditions—20th century.
Classification: LCC CT275.H5667 A3 2018 | DDC 305.38/2309764—dc23
LC record available at https://lccn.loc.gov/2017032065

Liveright Publishing Corporation
500 Fifth Avenue, New York, N.Y. 10110
www.wwnorton.com

W. W. Norton & Company Ltd.
15 Carlisle Street, London W1D 3BS

1 2 3 4 5 6 7 8 9 0

WITH THANKS TO CRUMB

Neither love without knowledge nor knowledge
without love can produce a good life.

—Bertrand Russell

CONTENTS

PROLOGUE

1989

My Uncle Cotton died out in East Texas, near
Huntsville. I found out through Alton that he had left us both
his old truck. Alton said he didn't have time to go get it, wasn't
worth the trip, so I took the bus from Austin to Hunstville and
my aunt Dee picked me up and gave me the title and Uncle
Cotton's truck, a blue 1979 F-250 Ford. The tires were worn,
it was a little battered, but it had a nice full headache rack
over the whole bed that could hold any paint ladders I had,
lumber or roller poles, and a lockbox in the bed I could put my
brushes and other tools and supplies in. I thanked my dad's
sister profusely, and she gave me a pan of her blackberry cob-
bler and I split back to Austin. The Ford was ten years old, but
it had low miles, didn't leak oil, and I finally had a halfway
decent ride.

I'd moved out of the rent house Susan and I had in Travis Heights, but she stayed. We were still seeing each other
here and there, mainly whenever she felt like it. I moved into
a fourplex atop a high hill off Ninth Street in Clarksville. It
was a nice, small efficiency on the second floor surrounded by

tall, ancient green live oaks. It was like a little tree house with big old double-hung sash windows on three sides, my view 180 degrees over South Lamar and all of downtown Austin to the east. I put my desk, typewriter, and the few books I had taken with me in the corner in front of the windows. I could look out across the green trees and buildings of the city as I wrote, typed, and listened to cassettes on a Sony Walkman I'd bought.

I didn't have a couch because Susan was so pissed when I moved out that she kept it. That was okay, but she also kept my entire album collection, and that was bad. I had hundreds of records, from sixties releases like the Doors' first album, or original, green Apple editions of the *White Album*, *Hey Jude*, old, original Stevie Wonder, the Supremes, Led Zeppelin, Pink Floyd, David Bowie, the Allman Brothers, the Isley Brothers, Marvin Gaye, Neil Young—all the music from the seventies—to Patti Smith, Laurie Anderson, Brian Eno, punk, new wave, Terry Allen, Doug Sahm, Texas country redneck rock, and many a local Austin band. It was a massive, eclectic mix of records from 1968 to 1989. Some of those albums had belonged to my extended family, but most of them had been my one great indulgence in life when it came to money. They represented so many days and years of good times as I had listened to them to escape from my daily reality as a child, as a teenager, and as a young man, listening to them while either drawing, or writing, or just sitting alone and thinking, watching the records spinning around on my turntable.

I went over to the house in Travis Heights then one day to load up my couch in the truck and get all my records, my turntable and speakers, but I found that Susan had changed the locks on the front and back doors. I also found out, when I called her that night, pissed off myself, that she had thrown away several stacks of my drawings and paintings, watercolors, pastels, that had been under our large bed. To be fair, she had called me first and asked me if she could get rid of all the drawings, or, really, she had said, "Do you want all this stuff, all these sketches, or *what*? You wanna just come get them? Because if not . . ."

I had foolishly said no at the time, I wasn't coming for them. I was trying to sound tough and casual, as though I didn't care, possessions didn't matter to me. Thinking it over later, I realized those charcoal, pen-and-ink, and pencil drawings, my pastels, my stacks of sketchbooks were so completely full of drawings that they represented hours, weeks, and years of my work and life. There were drawings in there I'd done of my mother and father when I was a boy, realistic portraits of my now-dead grandparents, or old girlfriends, landscapes of the Texas hill country and our home, still-life drawings from years of my father's enforced "drawing time" at my drafting table when I was a teenager, and some of my very best work, when I was finally getting some real instruction and developing skill in the advanced life-drawing classes I'd taken in college before I quit. It wasn't genius or anything, but it was irreplaceable, and I let her toss it all. I had grabbed only two of my paintings off the wall when I left, a bloody red acrylic portrait of Augusto Pinochet and a black-and-white-wash two-panel canvas painting of Robert Oppenheimer testifying before HUAC in the 1950s. I put them both in the one closet in my new apartment. Susan kept the portrait of Leonid Brezhnev though, or she said she did. I never saw it again.

My tree house was pretty empty then, but I liked it. I had no pets officially, but there was a stray, a cream-colored cat who started showing up occasionally, meowing outside my door on the balcony railing. This cream-colored cat began to come around a lot, and one day she walked in my open front door, took a look around, and ran back out. I always kept my door and windows open as I sat there in the evenings looking out at the trees and the tops of the buildings of Austin.

I was comfortable, but I suppose I was a little lonely too, and when the cream-colored cat came back the next time, I jumped up and got her a bowl of milk, and she lapped it all up. Before I knew it I was buying cat food, the cheapest dry stuff I could find, and when she showed up again, I put some out and she ate it and let me pet her. I did this for a few weeks, and we got friendlier and she began to trust me. I named her Sandy, and sometimes I would let her come in my place in the afternoon to sleep on the kitchen floor or clean herself, whatever, but I always kicked her out of the apartment at dark to go live out on the street as I didn't want her getting too comfortable. I didn't want a litter box or some cat I had to be responsible for, spraying the walls or sleeping on my bed at night.

OTHER PEOPLE

I had to get a job. In 1983 when I was twenty years old and a student at the University of Texas at Austin, I published one of my first short stories in a magazine. That story won a small prize, and I got some money for it. I thought, Man, this is gonna be *easy*, and I dropped out of college to write full-time. I didn't know then I wouldn't publish another word for fifteen years. Either way, I was quickly dead-ass broke.

Ronald Reagan had just become president. The UT campus was in the middle of Austin, up the hill from the tall, pink granite State Capitol at the top of South Congress. UT was a relaxed, liberal place when I arrived in 1981, where you could throw Frisbees on the long green lawn before the Tower and smoke dope in the afternoon and not get hassled, play with your dog, or just lie there in the grass and stare up at the sky instead of studying, which I did a lot. There was a mock South African shantytown some group had built on the West Mall, where students debated politics, the main two issues at the time, the need to free Nelson Mandela from prison and for Israel to quit killing so many Palestinians.

I'd come onto campus with the same long-haired, dope-smoking, country-boy Marshall Tucker Band look my friends and I'd had in high school, but I immediately dropped it when I discovered the whole punk rock scene in Austin. There was music everywhere, and my few new college friends and I went to punk clubs like Raul's on the Drag (Guadalupe Street, across from campus) or down to Liberty Lunch to see bands like Jerry's Kids, the Dead Kennedys, Circle Jerks, or Black Flag. We wore ripped jeans and white T-shirts on which we'd scribbled the words "Fuck Off" with Magic Markers, and considered ourselves hard core. We couldn't stand the new wave music that was also coming along, to the point that, one night, me and a couple of other punks saw the orange-haired lead singer from the group Flock of Seagulls walking down the Drag and almost beat the shit out of the poor guy. We ate speed, white crosses, and smoked clove cigarettes down at Les Amis, gabbing into the night, and were generally insufferable.

They closed down Raul's, and I got tired of the macho-mosh-pit bullshit and succumbed some to new wave anyway, or to more local Austin music and started hanging out at the Soap Creek Saloon to watch the Uranium Savages or bands at the small Continental Club, or Clubfoot downtown off Fourth Street, or we went up to a rectangular firetrap on Guadalupe called Antone's where you could get your boots shined and hear real, old blues musicians play. You could see the Clash for cheap down at City Coliseum, where we booed Stevie Ray Vaughan off the stage, or Elvis Costello or the Pretenders. Down at Clubfoot, one night you could be watching local acts like Joe King Carrasco, and the next night James Brown would be on stage with his cape, doing his whole deal.

We used to go down to Town Lake and swim in it. There was no Dell Mansion on Lake Austin. Texas Instruments was some company out in the country way up in North Austin off Highway 183. As far as I knew, they made calculators there. We went to Zilker Park in the summers to jump into Barton Springs, a clear, cold, blue-green, limestone-bed swimming hole as big as a football field, where women sat topless on the opposite bank and no one cared. There were still hippies in town, real ones, a little older now, and South Central Austin along Riverside and Lamar, South Congress, Oltorf Avenue— they were all cheap places to live, with neighborhoods like Travis Heights filled with small old inexpensive houses surrounded by a number of low-rent apartment units.

*   *   *

Almost overnight this weird, white Ronald Reagan wave hit UT. The campus was suddenly overflowing with Young Republicans who dressed and acted like Michael J. Fox in *Family Ties*, and a whole new set of frat boys and sorority girls were everywhere, too many for my tastes, yet another reason to get out of college. Even though the rest of the state was going into a recession, many people were now moving to Austin. Houston was nothing but a giant mass of people, traffic, concrete, mosquitoes, and flooding brown polluted bayous; Dallas, a nondescript big city sprinkled with rich white pricks, always either too hot or too cold up there. But Austin was still a small place, perched on the edge of the Hill Country, filled with old trees, clear creeks, blue lakes, and limestone hills, with the wide green Colorado River cutting right through the center of town.

The city was booming then, and the skies were filled with steel cranes, the streets suddenly lined with many more men and women in suits. I enjoyed watching the big-haired young women who seemed free and attractive and windblown downtown, all of them dressed in different colors, walking alone or in pairs. The businessmen seemed to travel only in groups of three or four or six, all white, all loud, all dressed alike in dark-blue suits, white shirts, the only spark of individuality an occasional odd-colored tie. When these men weren't marching by on the sidewalks they seemed to glide effortlessly past me in gigantic black Suburbans, an arm around the man sitting next to them, laughing and talking within an insulated cocoon.

*   *   *

I had been reading every book I could find and drawing everything I saw since I was a child. I'd always made the highest grades in school, eager to please my teachers, and eventually got myself an academic scholarship to UT Austin based on my transcripts, essays I had written, and my extensive drawing portfolio. My parents firmly expected me to become a successful artist someday, or a rich architect, a rich doctor, whichever came first or paid more. My older brother, Alton, was more of a typical Texas redneck, more so than me, I felt. My mother and father didn't expect much from him, ever, and they let him know it. I was the one who was supposed to do something with my life.

My parents had married very young due to my mother being pregnant with Alton when she was only fifteen. I came along just a year later. They had had it rough for a long time and were strict and rigid. My family, all we ever did, was mostly fight out there in our small house in the country. Or we did our chores, constantly, around the house and on the few acres of land my father owned, clearing cedar, cutting firewood, mowing pastures, weeding the gardens, or hauling hay. I always had some ass-busting job to do for as long as I could remember. I hated to work, but I was strong and did what I was told. Since I could also draw, my father turned that into another job, forcing me to start drawing at my desk every night for hours. He called it "drawing time" and said it could help me become a wealthy commercial illustrator or, even better, an architect. I had to do it after school every day, after my job at the grocery store, after my chores, sports practice, and homework, until one night I began to forget why I ever even started drawing in the first place.

*   *   *

I got back with my old girlfriend Susan Hampton in 1983, the year I quit college. We had been dating off and on since we were in high school in Cypress, a small town out in the Hill Country. Her mother, Betty Sue, was an attractive mostly retired actress from Texas. Susan's father was a former football player for the Los Angeles Rams named Dean Hampton, who had quit the game to become a successful novelist. I'd met Dean in 1978 when I was sixteen and started dating his daughter, at what turned out to be the height of his power, wealth, and fame.

When I first met Susan, she was unlike any other girl I'd ever known. She read books all the time, just like me. She loved movies as much as I did, but she had seen them from behind the scenes and wanted to be an actress herself one day, like her mother. Susan's music, her whole look and outlook, were still mostly stuck in the late sixties. Both of us felt we'd been born just a few years too late and had missed all the fun. I thought she was intelligent, more worldly than me, having moved into our small Texas town from Los Angeles. We had an identical, smart-ass take on our school, our town, our state, the country, everything. She and I would talk for hours into the night, sharing every intimate memory and detail about our families and pasts. I did everything a teenager could, every day and night, to try to get away to be with her.

Susan was tall, with thick, dirty blonde hair, blue eyes, full pink lips—her bottom one slightly larger, pouting above her chin. She had a disarmingly sweet and wholesome smile she could and would turn on to full power. Her parents often left us alone, and we would have sex in her bedroom while listening to albums late into the night, old ones like *Let It Bleed* or Fleetwood Mac's *Rumours*, which Susan wore out on her turntable. She was somewhat flat chested, which I liked, with a firm small ass, and a light brown bush of pubic hair I would bury my face in when she went down on me and we got into a sixty-nine. She had the same insatiable sex drive as I did. Though I'd had to beg my old girlfriend to just give me a bad hand job, Susan would slowly and deeply suck me off at lunch in my truck in the school parking lot, asking me to come into her mouth, swallowing as though she truly wanted all of it. We had sex anywhere we could for the first year we knew each other.

It was the first time I had ever experienced romantic love, had ever given myself over so completely to another person. Susan and I were also best friends. We had our little two-person clique and felt we were above most every other country yahoo student in the rest of the high school. One day though, in our junior year, Susan suddenly broke up with me with no warning, no signs at all of anything being wrong. I had always had girlfriends, and plenty of breakups, so it wasn't that big a deal. What was strange was how utterly cold she suddenly became toward me. She had made me feel so special and smart before, and yet, within a twenty-four-hour period, it was as if I were a complete stranger, a fool, and she completely ignored me. I was naive. I had thought we could at least still know each other, say hello in the halls or something, but no, she had become the Ice Queen and I ceased to exist in her eyes. She didn't even get another boyfriend.

I was baffled but also a horny teenager surrounded by beautiful country girls in our small high school. I figured, Screw this weird chick and started dating a couple of other girls. To my complete surprise, as soon as I went out on two or three dates with other girls, it was as if someone had switched a light back on in Susan's heart. Not only did she know me again, she threw herself at me so dramatically it was embarrassing. She wrote me dozens of notes and love letters every week, bought me gifts, albums, and for Christmas, a brand-new receiver, expensive turntable, and big Pioneer speakers, a whole stereo system. She called my house constantly, waited for me outside every class, asked me to come to her house again, and at one point she even befriended Alton to reach me somehow.

Alton had told me he thought Susan was "a snob" when he first met her. The first time she came to see our parents, they didn't like her either. They felt she was "too independent" and "spoiled." "It's like she thinks she's smarter than me," my father said. Plus she demanded way too much of my time, which my father felt belonged entirely to him. Alton didn't like her at all and didn't know (or maybe he did) how much Susan made fun of him for being ignorant in class, cutting him down to me in private, all of which I went along with, as I felt he was a bit of a dumb-ass too. But he was a sweet guy, more gullible than me, and when she befriended him, crying, asking for me to take her back, even Alton said I should give her another chance.

When we got back together, it was as if nothing had ever happened. We were having sex again every day. She was being normal and nice. It felt so good to be back in her favor, to have her complete attention, such blatant adoration, to have her listening to my every utterance and word. I fell in love with her even more than I had been before, which didn't seem possible. And then, three months later, she did it again: She abruptly broke up with me, I went out on a couple of dates with the tall, sexy drill-team leader, Tammy Ortiz, and fucked her in my truck one night, Susan prostrated herself before me, and we started all over. It was a mind game before I even knew what mind games were, but the sex was so good that in the end, I could never resist her. I always went back.

When I fell in love with Susan Hampton, I also jumped ship on my own family. I never wanted to be at my own house anymore. It suddenly seemed dull, and the fights between my parents had become so severe that either my father or mother was gone half the time, or my father's fights with Alton and me had grown even more physical and mean. He couldn't whip us; both of us were bigger than him now, but we were still afraid of this angry man and tried to stay as far away from him as possible.

I almost moved into the Hampton home, I was there so much. They had a large, open limestone-and-cedar ranch house on a high hill above the whole town of Cypress. Susan had a four-year-old little brother named Jason, and we often babysat him or took him down to swim in the blue creek that ran behind their land. I felt that Susan's parents were more laid back and much more interesting than my own. They smoked dope and had cool jobs, Dean writing his books and his wife, Betty Sue, still able to land an occasional acting job, mainly in commercials now.

More than anything, I was deeply impressed by Dean Hampton, a real writer. It felt good to have this intelligent, tough, sarcastic, and funny man take such a genuine interest in me. I did more talking than writing back then, telling Dean stories about my troubled family and life, and I can remember the real pleasure it brought me to make him laugh. He even encouraged me to write these stories down. One day, standing in his kitchen, he told me that my constant complaints about my school, my friends, and especially the stories about my family reminded him of J. D. Salinger, whose books I had just read for the first time and loved. It was pretty much the highest compliment anyone, especially a published author, could have possibly given me as a sixteen-year-old boy, and I really believed him.

Dean was interested in what I was reading, and we talked at length about books. He gave me many books from his own shelves, good authors to read, all of which I liked, including a first-edition orange-and-yellow hardback of Kurt Vonnegut's

Breakfast of Champions and a battered, black, dog-eared paperback of his favorite novel, *Under the Volcano* by Malcolm Lowry, a book he suggested I read at least twice to get it all, which I immediately did.

Dean told me hours of his own stories late into the night as I hung out at their house, not wanting to go back home where I would only get into trouble. He and Betty Sue let me crash on the couch in their living room or on a bed in the den. Dean always had trouble sleeping due to his many football injuries, including a twice-broken back, and he would wake me up sometimes at three in the morning as I lay on their couch, and he'd sit across from me as we watched old movies he had on video, some of his favorites like *The Wild Bunch* or *The Lion in Winter*. He knew every line of dialogue in the screenplays, the significance of every scene, and taught me how to appreciate different films, different directors, and their techniques.

Mostly he talked of himself. He told me of the harsh realities of playing in the NFL as a tight end, how it had ruined his enjoyment of the game as an amateur high school and then college football player. He said it had never been better than winning the state championship in his senior year in high school back in his home state of Ohio, or the bowl game, the national championship, he won at Ohio State. More than anything, he complained to me of his life right then, explaining how he really felt about the publishing industry, that he thought it was brutal and too commercial as football had become, angry with what his publishers expected from him as a writer.

I remember him telling me in 1979 how frustrated he felt after the major success of his first novel about football. Even though it had also been made into a profitable, popular feature film, he said he just didn't want to write about football. He said he wasn't even that interested in sports anymore. He talked of politics and history instead, and the political stories he wanted to write—investigative articles or novels on corporate and government corruption. He showed me a long detective novel he was working on, hundreds of typed pages, and he seemed crushed only a year later when it was repeatedly rejected and he was forced to write yet another book about football, in what became a series of less and less popular novels about sports, the only books his agent could sell or magazine articles he was paid to write.

* * *

My own father was a hard-ass who had always had a boss. He had worked at low-wage manual-labor jobs for many years of his life until, by working two jobs and putting himself through night school, he finally landed a well-paid white-collar position and started commuting to work at a large insurance company in Austin. He had convinced me that "real men" could still work with their hands and their backs though, a message thoroughly pounded into my head, and into Alton's, all our lives. I found it especially intriguing then that Dean Hampton, as a full-time well-paid writer, didn't really seem to work for anybody. For years my father had risen at dawn, gone off to a hard job to slave away for others, and come home every evening angry and tired. I was worried he was training me to do the same thing.

But Dean, he could sleep till noon, get stoned in the middle of the day, and then take a bunch of Dexedrine and codeine and write all night, standing up, writing by hand on long yellow legal pads at his lectern in the big Hampton den with its tall glass wall and deck looking out over the hills of Cypress. He could snort some coke and write for hours, or he would just stop when he didn't feel it, smoke a joint, and go see a movie. He'd get high and go outside and shoot off one of the many, many guns in his large collection or come home drunk at four in the afternoon, put on the Allman Brothers' first live album, *At Fillmore East*, turn up the volume, play air guitar wildly, and sing every word to "Whipping Post" as loud as he could. I was right there, and I watched him do all these things. I had never seen anyone so thoroughly and successfully be their own boss, with so much control over his own time, doing whatever the fuck he wanted, when he wanted, every day. I was seventeen years old. I forgot about that whole rich architect or doctor thing. And as I watched Dean Hampton at work and at play, I said to myself: Yes, yes, yes, *this* is the job, *this* is what I want to do.

By the time Susan and I got back together in '83, we'd had half a dozen dramatic breakups and reunions. Somewhat like us, her mother, Betty Sue, and Dean also had a volatile relationship, but it was much more violent, hard, and real. At that time, as I was quitting college, both Susan and her mother had gone into hiding, Susan down in San Marcos, her mom up in Austin. Betty Sue had finally worked up the courage to divorce Dean Hampton and had fled to live with an old close friend, a wealthy screenwriter and producer in Austin named Martin. I found out all of this by accident, as I had sworn off Susan for good once I'd gotten into UT and moved to Austin. It was an accident that we'd even found each other again.

Susan was working as a phone operator in San Marcos at

the small exchange there in town. I made a phone call from Austin to San Marcos one day and dialed the local phone company information line to ask for a number. I had no idea Susan was working there, and after the operator gave me my number, she paused, and before I could hang up, she said, "Jake?" I recognized her voice and said "Susan?" and neither one of us could believe it; it seemed like fate. She asked if she could call me back and I said sure, and when she did, we talked for hours. She drove to see me in Austin that same night, walked in the door of my apartment and we had sex on the carpet in the living room, talked some more, and went and fucked in my bed for an hour. She spent the night and never really left again.

Susan told me that her father had had a paranoid rage- and drug-fueled nervous breakdown after his latest book came out and failed at the same time her mother had filed for divorce. Dean Hampton was tall and carried guns on him at all times, at least two or three, a .38 pistol in an ankle holster, a Beretta automatic behind his back, or a heavy, silver .357 Magnum in a large shoulder holster beneath his left arm. Though the game of football had broken down his body, he was still a strong, imposing man. Worse, he was now dependent on opiates and cocaine and was threatening to do things like "knock out all of those pretty teeth I paid for, right out of Susan's fucking mouth!"

Betty Sue was a petite woman, and she was getting the worst of it, especially when Dean showed up and broke into their house in Cypress one afternoon. She said he picked her up by the throat and punched her in the stomach. The county sheriff came out, and Dean pulled a twelve-gauge pump shotgun on him. The old sheriff knew Dean well, they'd once been friends, and after he calmly talked him down, Dean spent a week in jail and had a restraining order put out on him. He had to leave the Cypress house for good and moved into a hotel off Oltorf and I-35 (not a mile away from my own apartment), where he had joint visiting rights to see his son, Jason, every week during the divorce.

Once Dean found out that Susan was living with me in Austin, he phoned me immediately, and he caught me off guard.

"Hey, Jake, how's it going?" He sounded friendly, the same old Dean.

"Okay, man."

"Listen, I need to talk to Susan, is that all right?" I looked at Susan, and she waved me off vigorously and mouthed the words "No way."

"Uh she can't talk right now, Dean. I'm sorry, but—"

"Yeah. I see. You're *sorry*. You know, I thought this might happen. I thought you might take their side. Actually, I *knew* you would take their side."

"Come on, Dean, what am I supposed to do? She's my girlfriend, and Betty Sue's her mother."

His voice grew hard and mean. "Listen to me, Jake. Listen to me very carefully, okay? All right?"

"Yeah, right."

"Don't you 'yeah right' me. Look, you are a man now, do you understand? You're not a little teenage jock anymore. And you better hitch up your pants if you wanna fuck with me, son. You got that? You're a grown man, and you are fucking with my life, my wife, and my kids."

"I'm not trying to fuck with your life."

"Jesus Christ, how naive can you possibly be? Don't you realize those two women are just using you? Jake, Betty Sue and Susan, both of those women are smarter than you and me *put together*. They are fucking black widows who eat men for breakfast. They are using you to try to *replace me* in my son's life, in Jason's life."

"What?"

"Come on, Jake, you think I don't know what's going on? Jason may only be seven years old, but he's a sharp kid and you think he's not gonna tell his father what his manipulative, shallow, lying little bitch of a mother is trying to do to me, his father, the only *one person* in *all* of this who really cares about him? He told me that they even had you taking baths with him and reading to him in the bathtub just like I used to. Are you gonna deny that?"

I stumbled briefly. They had asked me to do this once, and I'd felt uncomfortable when I did so out at the ranch house in Cypress. He was right; it was a pretty blatant replacement move, and I'd turned down both Betty Sue and Susan when they tried to get me to read to Jason in the tub again.

"No, I'm not gonna deny it, but yeah, that was uncool. It only happened once."

"So you *can* see it now. You *can* see how they are trying to replace me. And don't think I don't see how they're *both* using sex to manipulate you as well. I mean, we already know that Susan is a whore—"

"Hey, don't call her a whore—"

Susan began to flutter around me. "Hang up the phone, Jake. Hang it up."

I waved her off, getting pissed. "Listen—"

"You two were fucking so much under *my* roof in *my* house I told her I was going to have to give her away in purple."

"Yeah, she told me you said that a few years ago."

"Did you ever read her little diary that I told you about? Did you read about all the other guys she was fucking when she was fucking you?"

I could feel my ears turning red. I had read a few pages of her diary once in our senior year, and yes, she had been with other guys, but I'd been with other girls also. At the time it pissed me off so much that it led to one of our many breakups, which Dean knew well. I couldn't think of anything to say, and he rolled over me.

"You think I didn't see the way Betty Sue sat on your lap and put her arms around you and told you just how cute your skinny little ass was *all the fucking time*? Huh? Did that give you a hard-on?"

"Dean—"

"Honestly, you are going to tell me that you have *not* noticed how very much *my wife* flirted with you constantly and wanted to *fuck* you too?! *Are* you fucking her too, Jake? Has she gone that far yet? To get her way? Because she will. Betty Sue was fucking nigger football players the same week I married her ditzy ass. She sure as hell wouldn't hesitate to screw her daughter's boyfriend if it helped her out in a custody battle, which, once again, you so *naively* do not see. They are both *using you* to *replace* me and I am *not* going to let that happen! And you're not gonna do shit about it because *you* are a *coward*."

I stumbled again, taken aback. "I'm not a coward."

Susan was crying now, her hand to her mouth. "Please hang up the phone."

Dean laughed. "Jake, you had an ulcer at seventeen years old. And now you're what, only twenty-one and your fucking hair is falling out. You're afraid of your father; I know you are, you *told* me you were. You don't even know what you wanna do with your life. First you tell me you want to be an artist, then you wanna be a writer, and I heard you just quit college, that you can't even hack that. You need to grow the fuck up, man. But more than anything, you need to stay out of this custody battle or you *will* regret it. I can *promise you* that you will regret it."

I was finally getting my bearings back a bit, and my own voice took on a familiar edge I didn't like. I sounded like my father, and I spoke slowly: "Okay, tough guy. Are you *threatening* me now?"

His voice changed back to the person I had found so charming for years, and only minutes before. "No, no, no, no. Hey, Jake, come on, man. I'm not *threatening* you. I'm just trying to *warn* you about those two *women*. I'm trying to simply tell you that *they* are trying to destroy me and that I can guarantee they *will* destroy you."

"Is that right . . ." I lit a cigarette. " 'Cuz it sounds like you're trying to threaten me, that you're trying to scare me or something."

"Listen, I am not threatening you. I do *not* want to go back to jail, all right? I just got *out* of seven days in jail because Betty Sue said I hit her."

"Yeah, she told me you punched her in the stomach."

"*That's* what she told you?!" he said, with exaggerated disbelief. "See, man, this is what I'm talking about. Remember Betty Sue was *an actress*. You can't trust *anything* an actor *ever* tells you. The reality is that I tried to reach inside of the back door of the ranch house—you know, the patio door for the kitchen—and *she* is the one who shut the door on my hand. I mean, my fingers just barely brushed against her shirt, the front of this loose-fitting shirt she had on, and she calls the cops and turns that into an assault charge and a restraining order and seven days in jail, which crushed Jason. So no, I am *not* threatening you, or Susan, or Betty Sue, and I'd appreciate it if you didn't call the cops and say that I did. All right?"

"I don't need to call the cops on you."

"Good, that's good, Jake. Again, I just wanted to tell you to please, *please* be very careful right now. Be *very* careful."

"Yeah, right."

"Okay, and listen, you guys have a happy Easter. Tell Susan I said that: You guys have a happy Easter."

"Sure," I said and hung up, my stomach churning.

Susan looked at me and shook her head. "He's poisoned right now. Do you see what I'm talking about?"

"Yes," I said. "Yes I do."

*   *   *

I had been threatened more by my own father over the years, but it hurt to have Dean turn on me. He did scare me enough that I went to a pawnshop on the East Side of Austin, on First Street, and bought a .45 automatic, just in case he dropped by the apartment. I bought a box of bullets at Walmart. I got stoned, though, one day and took the gun apart to clean it, just as Dean himself had once shown me when he taught me how to shoot and care for such guns in high school. But without his help I couldn't put the gun back together and ended up taking it back to the pawnshop in pieces and lost some money.

Susan and I got married a few weeks later, in 1983, both of us now twenty-one. We had the ceremony in the living room of her "uncle" Martin, the successful old screenwriter and producer who had taken in her mother as his full-time secretary and personal assistant. He lived in the highest hills in Westlake, and it was an easy, fun wedding with only a few of our closest friends and relatives there. Susan's little brother Jason walked her down the improvised aisle to give her away to me. We were married by some old, smart, Austin stoner judge, and Susan and I said our heartfelt vows that we'd written ourselves. We kissed as everyone clapped, standing there in Martin's big living room looking down over the green, cedar-lined hills and valleys, the clear rivers and creeks that ran into Austin.

Dean called me again as soon as we got back to my apartment off Riverside. We were about to leave to go to South Padre Island on the Texas coast for a week to stay at a nice beach house a friend of Martin's owned for our honeymoon. We had scored two eight balls of good blow, had a bag packed, and were ready to walk out the door when I picked up the phone.

"Yeah?"

"Jake?"

"Dean?"

Susan yanked open the front door of the apartment. "Hang up the phone right now!"

"Jake," he said in an almost comically ominous voice, "now you *truly know* why you are a coward."

"Yeah, hey, Dean, I don't have any more time to listen to

your bullshit. You caught me off guard last time. But you can go screw yourself now."

"Okay, tough guy—"

"No, no, *you're* the tough guy."

"You two really think you're hot shit now, don't you? You think I don't see you guys snorting coke on *my* fucking bed, in *my* master bedroom in Cypress?"

"What are you, *spying* on us?"

"You and Susan are just the new hot couple now, aren't you? You both think you are *so* fucking clever. *So* fucking cute. And you, you just insulted me as a father, you insulted me pretty much more than any potential son-in-law ever could."

"What the hell are you talking about?"

"By not asking me for my daughter's hand in marriage."

"Is this before or after you threatened to knock all of her teeth out that you paid for?"

"I never said that. Susan just made that up."

"No, it sounds exactly like something you would say."

"And not only did you not ask me for my permission, my *approval* to let you marry my daughter, *then* you go and marry her in Martin's house, my best fucking friend, *and* you have the balls to rub it in by putting *my* son in your wedding. Was that Betty Sue's idea? Or was it Susan's? You can at least tell me that, because I know it wasn't *your* idea to have Jason walk her down the aisle. There's *no way* you thought of that."

"Dean, I gotta go."

"You know I'm living in a nice La Quinta Inn off I-35 now. This little place, it has a kitchenette, so I can cook food for Jason when he comes by. I'm watching *Apocalypse Now* again. I got it on tape. Remember when we all saw it together in San Marcos? Man, that movie blew me away. I gave you that book, *Dispatches*, by Michael Herr. Anyway, they got a nice big TV and VCR in this place. These divorce lawyers are bloodsucking parasites. The legal fees are killing me, so I'm renting it by the week."

"Oh yeah?" Once again he'd thrown me. He sounded stoned, lonely, and desperate.

"Yeah, it's not *quite* as nice as Martin's big house up in Westlake. Hey, just tell me this, Jake, is Betty Sue fucking Martin now also? My former best friend? And has Martin *really* just so *completely* attached himself to the Willie money train as it seems?"

"Seriously—"

"Okay, just tell me this, just tell me this: Does Martin carry a gun now? 'Cuz I know he didn't use to. Just tell me that, Jake."

"Man, I don't know. I don't think so, Dean. I doubt it. But really, we have to go."

"Where are you guys going? Are you going on your honeymoon?"

"Uh . . .," I paused, confused. "We . . . uh, yeah, we're going to the beach."

"What beach?"

"*That's it!*" Susan said and tried to grab the phone out of my hand. "Hang it up. *Now!*"

"I gotta go, Dean."

"Tell Susan I said hello, okay?"

"I will," I said, and hung up the phone.

* * *

By the time we got back to Austin, the custody battle for Jason had grown so intense that Betty Sue was almost collapsing from exhaustion. She was also having difficulty getting anyone in the Hill Country town of Cypress to testify on her behalf in the divorce proceedings. Dean had called up one of their best friends who was about to appear in court on Betty Sue's behalf, a young man named Bruce whom everyone, including my own family, knew as a gentle and almost stereotypically friendly country doctor. Days before Bruce was due to testify, Dean called him and begged him not to. When that didn't work, he showed up at Bruce's office one day and told him that he was going to kill him, "and then I will eat your guts out in front of your fucking children." Bruce backed out, and Betty Sue lost another witness as Dean's lawyers were going after her character for him to have sole custody of the boy.

Dean was soon scaring off his old friends in LA while pissing away his money on blow, legal fees, and limousines during the increasingly bitter divorce. I was at the ranch house in Cypress the day Bruce, the country doctor, came by to reluctantly tell Betty Sue he would not appear in court and that Dean had genuinely shaken him to his core. Losing her best witness seemed to be the last straw for Betty Sue, and she just stopped fighting.

Dean had run off most everyone in Texas as well, all their old friends, and though he was losing the house in Cypress and everything else in the divorce, he was not going to give up Jason, no matter what. One day he just took the boy, put him in his big, jacked-up '77 Blazer, and fled back to live again in his depressed and dying Rust Belt home town up in Ohio. And Betty Sue let them both go. Dean moved back in with his old mother, and the last I heard, Dean and Jason were both sleeping in the same small childhood room in the same little house that Dean had grown up in.

*   *   *

With the money Susan and I received from wedding gifts, our little bit of savings, my short-story check and the prize money, and even selling one of our cars, Susan's Toyota Celica, we proceeded to do nothing but drink and get high for months, well into 1984. We were mostly doing cocaine or, when the money got low, crank, crystal meth. We were still screwing every single day while crashing on friends' floors, moving back and forth from towns and cities all over Texas, but we always came back to Austin in the end.

I was writing feverishly, short stories and three-act plays, typing up page after page on my portable Smith Corona manual that came in its own carrying case that allowed me to write anywhere as long as I had some light, cigarettes, paper, and a bottle of whiteout. I sent out those stories and plays in SASEs every week. For some reason, anytime an editor, agent, or theater director accepted my work but then asked for the slightest change, I immediately pulled out of the magazine, or mainly it was the popular theater in downtown Austin, the Capitol City Playhouse, where I repeatedly fought with their main director over any form of compromise—or success.

Maybe part of me felt that success was, in some way, selling out. Or maybe it was because Susan and I really *did* feel we were just so smart and young, so clever and cute, that we needed no one and nobody could touch us. She signed her own typed letters to our friends with the line "Zelda and her husband," the fact that both writers, their marriage and careers, had come to such grim ends funny to us both.

It wasn't so funny when we found ourselves unable to pay the electric bill or the rent on a cheap one-bedroom apartment in the El Madrid, where we finally came down hard, on the edge of Travis Heights off South Congress and Riverside. I'd stopped talking to my parents, who hated Susan even more once I dropped out of college and married her. They were out as to hitting them up for any money. Betty Sue, her acting days over, was struggling to get on her feet working nonstop for Martin in Austin while trying to pay the mortgage on the old Hampton ranch house back in Cypress that she had won from Dean in the divorce. Dean was a bankrupt, well-armed, and still-pissed-off giant mess up in Ohio. Susan and I found ourselves then, one sad cold day, in the real world of adults— where no one gives a shit about you for the most part, no matter how cute you are—with no one else to rely on, certainly financially, but ourselves.

So yeah, I had to get a job. I decided on painting as I thought it would be much less noisy than some of the other industrial trades and seemed like the least work for the most money. With carpentry you actually had to make something and listen to hammering and loud saws at seven in the morning. Painting would be quiet, I thought.

Susan had found a grim job in a cubicle selling classified ads over the phone all day at the *Austin Times-Tribune*, which was just around the corner from our apartment in the El Madrid. The apartment complex had been built in the seventies but was already falling apart; stained green shag carpeting covered our floors, with lime-green, chipped, and speckled linoleum in the tiny kitchen, poorly patched thin Sheetrock walls, and an acoustic ceiling so thick and oversprayed it looked like yellow popcorn above our heads. All we had in there was a fold-out card table in the kitchen, a cheap Goodwill couch with two cardboard boxes in front of it that Susan had duct-taped together and put Con-Tact paper on to make a coffee table. We had a large Sony though, that her mother had given us, Dean's old TV, and his heavy VCR. In the bedroom we had a box spring and mattress sitting on the floor, surrounded by all our clothes, shoes, papers, books, magazines, and whatever clutter of crap we had left after our months of nonstop traveling and drinking and drugging.

We only had the one car now, mine, a battered, light-blue, two-door '72 LTD with a ripped blue vinyl roof and no side windows. I'd gotten the car along with some cash by trading, cutting, and selling more than an ounce of good coke through a dealer friend of mine. I had to drive Susan to work every morning. I remember her first day, that first morning, dropping her off. She didn't want to get out of the car, so we sat and talked for half an hour. Then, just before eight:

"I have to go in now."

I gave her a light kiss. "I'm sorry, babe."

"Me too."

She got out of the car and started walking toward the big white building. She stopped on the steps and turned and waved good-bye. I waved back and felt like I was abandoning her.

*   *   *

I picked the biggest paint contractor in town out of the phone book and called them for a week from a pay phone near our apartment. It said in the yellow pages they painted cars, residential, custom homes, commercial buildings, everything. They finally let me come down and fill out an application. I made up three years of experience at three imaginary paint companies in Houston. The owner of Austin Paint and Spray Company, Tim Wilson, called me into his office. He was from Alabama, in his thirties, short, with a huge gut and an old-fashioned flattop head of hair that had already turned solid gray. I'd cut my own hair and was very clean-cut and shaven, lying rapidly about how much I wanted to work for him. Tim mentioned the Austin real-estate boom and that Austin Paint and Spray, or APS, as everyone called it, would soon have more work than they could handle. He didn't seem to believe my experience, but he hired me at $7.50 an hour.

*   *   *

We met in North Austin in an industrial area above Highway 183 covered with giant chain-link-fenced parking and storage lots, the fence tops lined with curls of razor wire, the lots filled with work trucks, manufacturing materials, stacks of sheet metal and silver conduit, walls of metal pipes and fittings, and back-to-back metal prefab buildings and warehouses. All the APS painters sat in our little tin building every morning from seven to eight, waiting for Tim to give us our assignments. All of us smoked, so the room was always hazy and smelled of tobacco and paint thinner. I usually read the paper, the front page, first section, and sat in the corner trying not to talk to anybody.

There were two men who were the most vocal in the room: Jesse and Tyler. Tyler was a tall curly-headed guy from West Texas. He was missing his two front teeth and covered in scars and tattoos, Bugs Bunny on his left forearm and the Tasmanian Devil on the right, flipping you the bird. I guess because I was the youngest and quietest person in the room, Tyler picked me to listen to his exploits first thing every morning.

"I had this bitch last night I met down at Antone's. She was married an' I got 'er inerested in me when I got up onstage with Robert Earl an' I started playing my banjo. She wanted me, man. She liked my pickin'. She said she also saw me down at the Kerrville Folk Festival. Anyway, I got 'er out t' the truck an' this bitch was fine, I mean she was good-lookin' an' ready to fuck an' just when we was gettin' in my truck she starts pukin', just pukin' all over the place. I pushed her outta the truck an' said, 'Bitch, if you're gonna get sick, please do it in the parkin' lot an' not in my truck.' So she pukes it all up an' says, 'Okay, let's go,' an' I told her, 'You know, I think I'm ouyta the mood now, but get on in here an' we'll go on to my house.'"

I never even looked at him. I kept reading the front section, turning the pages.

"An' so—come on, man, listen! So I got her home an' fucked her an' she was all right but she just kinda laid there, I think she was out, but I fucked her anyway. She had all these blue ducks on her panties an' I took her panties off an' added 'em to my panty collection. You still haven't seen my panty collection, you gotta see it. You wanna see it?"

"What are you collecting panties for?" I asked him.

Tyler looked at me, confused.

"He wears them," somebody said.

"I have to collect 'em to remind me of each bitch I've fucked. Now listen. So I finally passed out an' I wake up in the night 'cuz I'm gettin' all wet. I look over at that woman an' she's wettin' the goddamn bed! I pushed her out an' said, 'Shit honey, the bathroom's right there.' She just stood up, though, and pissed herself right there on the floor."

"She sounds like a nice girl."

"Oh yeah, she was fine lookin'."

Jesse was the other talker. He'd fought in Vietnam and discovered heroin there. He had long black hair, a beard, and a giant tiger tattoo running down his right arm. Jesse would mix a large amount of methadone into his coffee every morning, and it really got him going. He was intelligent, but over the years a number of things had twisted his mind.

"Now look," he said. "I'm a liberal man, don't get me wrong, but it's just that the Vietnamese have no place in this country. I'm sorry, but I know 'em, and they're fucking scum. My landlord, who is this fucking schizophrenic nut-ball who can't decide how she wants to deal with our relationship, rents part of my duplex out to a fucking half-Vietnamese, half-American family. Right next door. They have two little Vietnamese girls so, shit, I try to be nice to them. They come by all the time and want to talk, they're about nine and twelve, and so they're bothering me and I give them some coins as a present; my father was a numismatist and I have this very valuable coin collection, and I give them two silver, real silver, dollars that are very fucking old that my goddamn father's father gave him, which he gave to me, and the two little sweeties run off and they come back and say, 'Look, Uncle Jesse, we bought four candy bars.' And I just froze and I said, 'You didn't use your very special silver dollars, did you?' and the oldest one says, 'Yes, and I got a Hershey's with almonds,' and I wanted to say, How would you like a foot rammed up your cunt, you stupid fucking kid?! That was very valuable, worth much more than a Hershey bar, worth much more than you, so how would you like me to ram my fist into your little twelve-year-old cunt? Huh? Do you see what I'm talking about now? The Vietnamese are fucking idiots."

I didn't really want to work with these guys, but of course Tim sent me with them. Since I didn't have much experience, they were putting me in a commercial building downtown with the hard-ass foreman, Big Jim.

Big Jim was a tall and big person from Alabama who'd gone to high school with Tim and thus was his right-hand painter. Jim was a nice-enough guy, though extremely dull. Every morning he would sit in the shop reading nothing but the food ads in the paper, or stacks of food circulars he'd received in the mail, marking down all the prices, adding up the discounts, talking with open anticipation of an upcoming sale on pork chops, Wonder Bread, or salami.

* * *

That first day, that first year, was terrible. Big Jim got in his old El Camino and told me to follow him to a new building going up at 301 Congress. I got into my '72 LTD with no side windows. Tyler got in his beat-up truck covered in bumper stickers: "I'm a Picker," "Honk if you love Banjos," "Follow me to the Kerrville Folk Festival." Jesse got in his old van, and we followed Big Jim downtown.

Big Jim wanted a lot of paint put up on those walls, and there were many walls and many floors in that building. It was fairly easy for me to learn how to slap it on by watching the other painters, and eventually I knew what I was doing. The main problem was time slowing to a muddy, sandy, wheel-halting, mind-numbing standstill. Jesse and Tyler talked to me all day, both men that certain type of talker-worker, a person who gabs constantly to divert your attention from their mediocre abilities. I preferred to work silently, letting my mind wander to some story or a play I'd been working on the night before, or to dreams of fame, practicing my visit to a TV talk show or my acceptance speech for the Oscar for my original screenplay, thanking the academy and pretending I wasn't where I really was.

Tyler sang country songs all morning. Or he explained his tattoos and scars: "I got this one after I got outta Huntsville. See, I shot my brother, the cocksucker—but he shot me through the neck." He pointed to a white round scar over his trachea and another wide scar on the back of his neck. "I didn't kill him, though. I got this one from a knife fight. Somebody shot me right here. . . ."

I soon realized that Tyler saw himself primarily as a country outlaw, and I had no doubt that, drunk on a Saturday night in an East Texas bar—or any bar—he was dangerous. But during the day he was a lazy painter and scared of his boss, his girl-friends broke up with him regularly, and he had no money. Tim and many others at APS thought he was a fool. And now, though he was only forty, he was developing some sort of Parkinson's disease, and his head was starting to shake back and forth all the time as were his hands, a bad condition for painting as well as banjo picking. Tyler's favorite saying was, "I'm a man, goddammit! I told her 'I'm a man.'" Or "Tim can't talk to me that way, I'm a grown man!" There was nothing I could do but listen. I was trapped for nine hours a day.

Jesse, flying on methadone, explained his life to me, though he could never get his stories straight. One day he was a paratrooper with two hundred jumps, the next he was an explosives expert or a tunnel rat. Some days he was a sniper. More than half the men in the shop were vets from a variety of wars, though few spoke of their experiences. Jesse was never shy. He, too, showed me his scars, two long white worms on his back.

"Those were from a VC sniper. I killed two guys from the front, and this fucker was hiding somewhere and shot me in the back twice. The bullets missed my spine by a fraction of an inch."

Or he spoke of prison. "They got me for transporting dynamite across state lines. I went to a federal penitentiary after that one. I tell you, if you ever commit a crime, make sure it's a federal offense. The fed is much better than state prison. I was in a state pen for years, and the thing that was so terrible about that is that state is full of a lot of incredibly stupid people who actually enjoyed being in prison in some weird way. They're too fucking stupid to function outside in society. They need to have a roof over their heads, food served to them, somebody to tell them what to do and discipline them, just like Daddy did. There is no way I'll ever go back to state, fuck that shit. Besides, I'm gonna kick 'done this year."

I kept painting, rolling my wall. "Oh yeah?"

"Yeah, it's just getting too fucking expensive. You know this piece-of-shit country is totally fucked. In England they just give the stuff to junkies for free. They have clinics, and the government just doles it out. It's legal, it's sane, and it's humane. Nobody wakes up and says, 'I want to be a fucking junkie.' It just happens one day and you are and you need more and you can't fucking find any and you have to drive down to San Antonio and I feel like I'm gonna die and I'm trying to wait in line and pay for this shit every fucking week down at the VA hospital. That new senator, Phil Gramm, that weasel was out on the Capitol steps the other day talking about some shit, and I went down there and I'm sorry, I apologize, but I just got pissed looking at that Capitol and all those politicians whose salaries are paid for by my payroll taxes and I started yelling, 'Hey! What about the Vietnam vets and the methadone program, Senator Gramm?! What about the methadone program, you fucking bastards! You never do shit for a vet!' And then just because I was yelling a little bullshit, these cops come running up and haul my ass away. You might notice at any event anywhere in this city, anywhere in this fucking country, there's cops with guns to come haul you away. You watch, you just make a little noise, you just disagree with this government, never mind disobey them, and see how fast a cop sits on your back and throws you in jail just like the Soviet Union, the Gestapo, the police, police fucking storm troopers, coming into your home to haul you away in the middle of the night . . ."

When lunch finally came, Jesse and Tyler and I went down in the freight elevator and stepped out on Congress Avenue. We walked down the sidewalk in our paint-spattered whites, and I grabbed a burger at Wendy's with the convicts. We rode the elevator back up, sat down on the hard concrete floor of

301 Congress and ate for our thirty minutes of freedom. Big Jim, our foreman, would often give me some little tidbit of wisdom. He was eating raw jalapeños and sausage.

"Say, you know how I got rid of my hemorrhoids, Jake? You know the best way to do it?"

I ate a French fry. "No."

"I'll tell you the best way: jalapeños."

"Oh yeah?"

"No shit. Mine were really bleeding bad one day, right through my pants, so my old lady went out and bought all of these jalapeños and I just ate 'em, one after the other, until I was full. The next day I had the shits real bad, these burning green jalapeño shits, but somehow it just cauterized my asshole and that was it. I've never had my hemorrhoids bleed again."

"That's interesting, Jim."

By five o'clock I was thoroughly exhausted. I'd been wrong about painting being quiet. The sound of all the other trades, sawing steel, shooting charges to set walls into the concrete, table saws ripping wood, air compressors running, carpet men yakking, electricians yelling to one another, supervisors yelling at everybody, the incessant jabbering of my coworkers, plus the fumes from the paint all gave me severe heartburn, forcing me to pop Rolaids all day.

At around five-thirty or so I drove over to Riverside to pick up my wife.

Whenever I picked her up, she was very tense and worn out.

"That was nine hours of my life wasted."

"Is it bad in there?"

"The supervisors are morons, and I have to sit there and not only listen to them, I have to do what they say. My boss is this idiotic frat boy who cannot even spell, I mean he can't spell 'Wednesday' or—he just can't spell. He tells my immediate supervisor what to do, and she tells me what to do."

"How's she?"

"I think she's insane."

"Really?"

"Completely, irrevocably. Probably a schizophrenic."

"And she's your boss."

"She'll be running the major part of my life now, and God, the girl next to me—"

"What?"

"I think she mentioned her bowel movements at least ten times today. Everything's diarrhea this and constipation that at eight o'clock in the morning. I can't stand it. I gotta sit there all day on the phone taking classified ads. I think there's maybe two normal people there. The nicest, smartest person seems to be my trainer for the main phone bank. Her name's Norma, and she's pretty cool, she doesn't take the job too seriously. Everyone else is a brain-dead robot slave."

"I'm sorry."

"But Norma seems nice."

"That's good."

"Yeah, I guess."

*   *   *

If I was late from the paint shop, if I missed her, Susan had to walk home. When I reached El Madrid, I sometimes walked over to apartment 103 to get her. Dwayne Coleridge lived in 103. Dwayne was a forty-three-year-old film professor at UT. He was also an acting teacher, a writer, a painter, a musician, a playwright, and a poet. He'd befriended us one day out by the apartment pool, and now he and Susan were close buddies. I'd walk into 103 and find them sitting at the table doing the I Ching.

"Dwayne just did my numerology chart," Susan said happily, puffing on a Winston Light. "Do you want us to do yours?"

"No, that's all right."

Dwayne stroked his handlebar mustache and lit a cigarette. "Can I get you a beer?"

"Sure, thanks."

He stood up and brought me a Shiner. I opened the beer and drank, looking around the room. Dwayne had our same shitty shag carpeting, but his apartment was larger and much cleaner than our own, with nice comfortable chairs, a big new couch, new TV, fully filled bookshelves, and thick wooden tables with way too many candles in ornate holders and Hindu goddess sculptures, neatly arranged, on every surface. His walls were covered in oddly proportioned, pretentious paintings, mostly of one man with thick black curly hair and a big mustache (Dwayne) always with one noticeably different naked woman, both of them in nude silhouettes, staring up at multicolored triangles, circles, or half-moons and stars, Lucky Charms, whatever the hell it was they were throwing into the air.

I tipped my beer at the largest canvas above his couch. "Nice paintings, Dwayne."

"You think so? I'm still experimenting, obviously."

"Right."

Susan fiddled with her numbers, astrology charts, the I Ching book.

"How was work?" she asked me, not looking up.

"Boring, mindless, terrible."

Dwayne took a sip of coffee. He drank gallons of it. "Another good day?"

"Another great day. How was yours?" I asked Susan.

"It was all right. Norma's getting promoted, so I'm going to move into her bigger gerbil box and work with her more, still taking calls but making some, too."

"Well, that's good news. I guess."

"Yeah, I might even get a raise."

"Great."

"You sure you don't want me to do your chart?" Dwayne asked.

"Nah, thanks. That's okay."

"This is really interesting," Susan said. "You can learn things from this."

"About your future?"

"Somewhat," Dwayne said.

"Specifically?"

"Pretty close," Dwayne said. "It all depends on how you go into it."

"Right."

We sat at the table. Susan frantically wrote down and added numbers on her numerology charts. I saw a slight grind working in her jaw and knew she must have done a little crank again with Norma at work. She and Norma had started to do a couple of small bumps a day to get them through the long boring afternoons on the phones taking calls all day, wearing their little headsets in their cubicle. I pulled out a cigarette, and Dwayne lit it.

"So what did you do today?" I asked Dwayne.

"Well, I wrote a song."

"Really?"

"You want to hear it?"

"Uh—"

"Sure," Susan said.

Dwayne reached back and picked up a guitar off the floor. He strummed and sang a song I'll never hear again, hopefully. We said we liked it and got up and left.

*   *   *

We were down in 103 one night with Dwayne. He was working on a movie at the time. "It's a Western detective story," he told me.

"What's it like?" I asked.

"Well, if Ingmar Bergman made a Western this is what it would be like."

"Is that right . . ." I lit a cigarette.

"It's got everything, though, violence, sex scenes."

Susan looked up from her chart. "Sex scenes?"

"Nothing very explicit," Dwayne said. "I'm not going to show them actually doing it, the two main characters."

"Why not?" I asked.

"It'll give the movie an X rating, for one thing."

"So?"

"It could be a problem with distribution, but, uh, I personally don't have a problem with it."

We smoked and had a few beers. Dwayne played his guitar and then turned on the TV. He had cable, fourteen channels, and switched the little box to the Playboy Channel. There were two people fucking, but it wasn't hard core.

"See, it's something like this," Dwayne said, "except even less. Probably not as much ass or titty. There is a scene in my film though, where a guy sniffs his wife's panties to see if she's been cheating."

"Oh?"

"Did you know Dwayne went to the Iowa Writers' Workshop?" Susan asked me.

"Oh yeah?"

"I'm afraid so," Dwayne said.

"Did you like it?"

"It was great. You can talk to a bunch of other writers and get a feel for each other, learn from each other. There were also some great teachers there. Nelson Algren and Kurt Vonnegut."

"Really? Kurt Vonnegut?"

"We had quite a few of the big postmodernists there. Donald Barthelme, John Barth. I started writing my film there."

Dwayne stood up, excused himself, and went into the other room. Susan, pencil to paper, worked on another cryptogram. That was her and Dwayne's main pastime: cryptograms, cigarettes, and coffee. What else were they doing down there? I didn't know, but Dwayne didn't seem to have a chance with his handlebar mustache and guitar.

"Let's go home."

Susan looked up. "Why?"

"I don't know," I whispered. "I think we're about to hear all about Dwayne's little movie."

"I've already heard it," Susan whispered.

"Is it going to be good?"

"It sounds terrible."

"Uh-oh."

"He said we could work on it. Carrying equipment around or something on the set. Be part of the crew."

"No thanks."

"You really don't want to?"

"How much are they paying?"

"Uh, nothing. I think you get a part of the profit if it's a big hit."

"Yeah, right."

"Okay, I'll tell him no. He wants me to go with him tomorrow night to see the Baba's daughter though."

"Who's that?"

"She's a holy woman from India. The successor to Baba, and she's coming to Austin. I think she's very intelligent. Norma and my mother are going. Do you want to come? My mom wants you to go with us."

"Betty Sue said that?"

"She thinks it'll be good for your stomach, your heartburn."

"Do I have to take off my shoes and sit on the floor?"

"You're not coming."

"Okay."

We sat silently for a minute. I looked at the TV and at Susan.

"Guess what else?" Susan asked.

"There's more?"

"Dwayne's giving me acting lessons for my birthday."

"Is it your birthday?"

"They're worth about three hundred dollars."

"Who told you that?"

"I think I'm going to take them."

"For how long?"

"Four weeks. He gave me the course outline and description. It's up in our apartment."

"Well, that's really sweet of him."

"It is," she whispered. "He's a genuinely nice, gentle person, so don't be a jerk."

"I'm not being a jerk."

"Just don't make fun of my acting classes please."

"I'm sorry. I didn't know you were so sensitive about it. I didn't even know you still wanted to be an actress."

"I don't. Or maybe I do. I don't know. It just sounds like fun, all right? I just want to do something, and it's free and no big deal, okay?"

"Sure, have fun."

Dwayne came back into the room and handed me a stack of papers. "This is a short story I wrote when I was at the Iowa Writers' Workshop. Go ahead and take it with you and read it."

I gave Susan a look and said, "Oh, thanks, Dwayne."

"We're going to go up now," Susan said quickly.

"Okay, no problem. Let me know what you think of that story, Jake."

"Sure. And listen, uh, thanks for giving Susan those acting lessons as a present. That's nice of you."

"Oh, hey, no problem. It's my pleasure. The more students the better. In fact, I'd be glad to have you in the class too, Jake. Frankly, I think you might have some potential as an actor."

"I think I'll stick to watching TV and painting houses."

"The offer's open any time."

"Thanks."

"I'll see you kids later."

Susan gave him a peck on the cheek. "Bye, Dwayne."

We walked upstairs, smoked a joint, and lay down on the floor on a blanket with pillows in front of the TV. I read Dwayne's story. Susan watched *Flashdance* on cable. I pointed to the young actress, Jennifer Beals, who was dancing on a chair.

"Maybe you could be like her someday."

"Someday."

"You really think Dwayne can teach you anything about acting?"

"Sure, and it'll be fun. The class is mostly made up of young girls—"

"Of course."

"So I could make some friends, maybe. How's that short story?"

"It's all right. You wanna read it?"

"No. What's it about?"

"Um, a guy who sounds suspiciously like Dwayne goes to Hollywood and ends up sucking some producer's dick and then the producer sucks his dick and then the producer dies, and this Dwayne-like person with curly hair and a handlebar mustache who is not Dwayne, though, realizes at the producer's funeral that Hollywood sucks, literally."

"Is it bad?"

"Actually it's pretty good. If I were him, I'd give up the Western detective movies and terrible love songs and write short stories."

"Well, I like him. I'm going to the classes."

"Don't let me stop you."

"I won't."

* * *

Susan went to her acting classes and was gone about three hours a night every week, making new friends, jumping around on a stage, pretending. I was getting bored sitting on the ratty couch watching videos, masturbating, smoking, drinking, and staring at CNN. It was 1984, and while she was out one night, I sat there and watched Ronald Reagan get reelected. I had voted after a full day of work, painting the exterior of a large home in West Austin. It had been a huge pain in the ass, that vote, since they didn't really want you to vote anyway or otherwise they'd make it a holiday, or at least set it up on the weekends. By the time I got to the small church in Travis Heights where we voted, it was getting dark and I had to stand in a long line for hours before I voted for Mondale.

By the time I got home and turned on the big Sony TV, NBC was already calling the whole election for Reagan even though the polls were still open out in California. All the anchormen were falling all over themselves with Reagan's landslide victory, going on and on about the "positive mandate" he now had to fuck up the country even more than he had already with his deregulation and bullshit, piss-down, trickle-down economics, where he slashed taxes for the richest people in America promising that the rich 1 percent would pass down the millions they made on their money to the rest of us rather than buy another new yacht or stash their cash in Switzerland and a post-office box in the Bahamas. Worse, what really pissed me off, was that he was canceling out all those hours I had just waited in line to vote for the other guy after nine hours of work in the hot Texas sun.

I couldn't watch any more of the Reagan coronation. I turned off the TV, smoked another joint, had a few beers, and went driving around. Who knew when Susan would be home, or what she was doing. I found a massage parlor in central Austin called Body Works and parked the car. It was a small wooden house atop a hill at the end of Twenty-Fourth Street where it met Lamar, across from Pease Park. There was one neon sign above the front door that flashed on and off in letters of blue light: "Body Works. . . . Body Works. . . ." I walked up to the little brown house and knocked on the door. An old Asian woman answered.

"Can I help you?" she asked.

"Yes, I'd like to get a massage."

"Come in."

I walked inside. Three Asian girls were sitting on a couch. They wore leotards and were watching *Dynasty* on a big color TV. The ugliest one stood up and walked over to me. She had on a light green gown over her black leotards. She had large breasts, but her face looked like it had been stepped on, and her eyes were crossed.

"No, no," I said. "I'm sorry. I want her." I pointed to a young girl sitting on the middle of the couch. She stood up, and I saw she was very short, maybe four feet eleven. Her hair was shoulder length, black, her body was perfect, and she had a pretty face.

"Her?" the old woman asked.

"Yes."

The woman gestured to a rate chart on the wall and

explained the charges in broken English. I picked the forty-dollar, one-girl, thirty-minute rate and paid her. The small prostitute then led me down a hall and through a door with hanging beads on the other side. She sat me down in a chair and said, "I'll be right back. Get ready, okay?"

"Okay."

I watched her walk back through the beads, staring at her ass. I looked around the room. It was dominated by a large water bed. There were two full-length mirrors on either side of the bed and small tables with dim lamps on them, their shades dark red. Several candles burned on the tables. A heavy blue curtain covered the large windows. There was a battered dresser next to the recliner I sat in.

After a few minutes, the girl came into the room. She was wearing a white towel around her body and acted surprised. "How come you not ready?"

"What?"

"How come you not take your clothes off?"

"I'm sorry, I'm a little drunk."

"What's wrong with your eyes?"

"I've got allergies."

"My name's Kim."

She knelt down in front of me and started untying my dirty work boots. She reached up to my crotch, slowly rubbed, and I got an erection.

"You like me?" she asked.

"Yes I do."

"You come see me anytime. I like you."

"Great."

She was having trouble untying my boots. Her towel

kept slipping off, and her fingers fumbled with the paint-caked laces.

"Where are you from, Kim?"

"Korea."

"How long have you been in America?"

"One year."

"Do you like it here?"

She looked up at me from the floor. Her black eyes locked on mine. It was a stupid question.

"It's okay. Sometimes good, sometimes bad."

"Right."

"Okay," she said loudly and smiled. She had my shoes untied. I slipped them off, stood up, and took off my pants and shirt. I pulled Kim up and said, "Let's get in the bed."

I lay on the water bed, and Kim sat next to me. She picked up a bottle of some mint-scented oil and rubbed it over my chest, and I began to relax. When she reached my erection, she soaked it with lotion and stroked slowly. She started to suck me off, and I watched her in both of the mirrors. From one side I could see her little ass, while the other mirror reflected her head bobbing up and down. I must have moaned because she stopped and said, "Don't come."

"Okay."

"You need rubber?"

"No, no."

"Yes, you need a rubber."

"Okay."

"When you come to see me, say you want one. Always tell me, and I get one for you. Always tell me."

She opened a drawer in one of the nightstands and took

out a condom. She opened it and put it on me. I lay there. Kim looked at me, confused, and opened her arms. She smiled sweetly and said, "Here I am."

"Come get on top of me."

"You want to fuck me?"

"Yes, right now."

She lowered herself on my cock slowly, and I watched in the mirrors. "It's good," she said. "You can fuck me."

Her ass was so small I could cup it in my hands. It felt strange but good. Kim began to hump on me very hard. I watched her ass move up and down in the mirrors. She kept kissing me all over the face and neck. I hesitated at first and then started kissing her back. We moved our tongues into each other's mouths, and I started sucking on her nipples and kissed her face and neck, tasting fresh mint. I came inside her, and the orgasm lasted a long time. She kept on fucking me, moving faster. I lay back, pressed her ass down, and moved her whole small body along mine. Her mouth was next to my ear, and I heard her moaning very quietly and intensely for several seconds. When she was through, we held each other and kissed a little more. After a little while she asked me quietly, "Are you through?"

"Yeah, that was great."

She stared at me. "I like you a lot," she said.

"I like you too, Kim."

"You come see me?"

"Yes."

"Anytime you come see me, I'm here. If you need a rubber, ask me and I get it for you."

"Okay."

She climbed off me, opened a drawer, and started putting

on another black leotard. She wouldn't stop looking at me and smiling. I got up and put on my clothes, and she ran over and hugged me. It was a very tight hug, and she wouldn't let go.

"I like you," she said. "I like you."

I hugged her lightly and tried to move away. She hung on and smiled at me. "I like you. You come see me?"

"Yeah, I'll be back."

"Anytime. Please. . . ."

It was the way she looked up at me. She was so small, like a little kid.

"I gotta go, Kim."

She let go of me, and I followed her through the beads and back down the hall. The other girls were still lying on the couch staring at the TV. A big old fat guy was standing by the rate board with a fat woman with greasy brown hair and acne. The old woman was explaining the rates to him.

"I want my wife to watch," the man said. "But I shouldn't be charged for her. . . ."

Kim opened the front door and hugged me again. "You come see me."

"I will. Good-bye."

"Bye-bye."

I walked to the LTD and got in. I sat and stared at the cracking dashboard. I heard cars driving down Lamar, saw the soft dim light coming from Body Works. I started up the car and drove home.

* * *

It seemed all we could ever rouse ourselves to do anymore was get stoned and go see a movie. Sometimes we saw four a week, just about everything that came out in the multiscreen places, it didn't matter what it was, just two hours of something. One night though, our old friend Pat came into town, and we decided to go out to a bar. Pat had a gram of good coke with her, and we did some at the apartment before we left. She told us that her and her boyfriend's relationship was strained.

"Corky's fucking this other girl right now," Pat said.

"How rude," Susan said.

"It is. It wouldn't be bad if she was halfway decent, but she's an ugly pig. I don't know what he sees in her. He's being a real asshole."

"Did he finish law school yet?" I asked.

"I don't know. I don't really give a shit. You know he didn't even come to my abortion?"

"Where was he?" Susan asked.

"He was off with her. I mean, he paid for it, but the least he could have done was take me down there and help me. Instead he went to see a Crosby, Stills & Nash concert."

"Crosby, Stills & Nash?"

"I know—he goes and sees a shitty concert with her. What an insult. I left him a terrible letter. I really gave him hell. I said, while you were playing grab-ass with that airhead bitch in Austin I was getting your baby sucked out of me in San Antonio."

"That oughtta get him."

"What a prick," Susan said.

"No shit, and there were all these protestors down there, these stupid Christian assholes, and this lady was begging me not to go in. I felt like slapping her. I'm really pissed at him."

We did some more coke and got in Pat's car and left. None

of us had any money for drinks so we drove to a nearby bar on the UT campus called the Cowboy Café. We parked, went inside, and since it was so late they just let us in. B.W. Stevenson was up on stage singing old songs. The place was packed with earnest people listening to the music. Susan found a table in a corner of the room with one guy sitting by himself. He was an old South Austin hippy with long hair in a ponytail and a big drooping mustache. Susan asked very sweetly if we could share his table, and he said sure and pulled out a chair. Susan sat next to him, and Pat and I sat together. BW sang, and Pat and Susan talked with the hippy guy and somehow mentioned that we didn't have any money but would all love a drink. The guy brightened to the idea.

"Hey, I'll buy you guys a drink. What do you want?"

"What are you having?" Susan asked.

"Uh, a Long Island Tea. That okay?"

"Are they strong?" Susan asked innocently.

"Oh yeah," the guy said and smiled. "Let's go."

He and Susan went to the bar. Pat and I listened to BW and clapped. Susan and the hippy came back with our drinks. We finished them off quickly, and he offered to buy us more. Sure, thank you.

After an hour and three more drinks, Pat and I were leaning together. Susan and the hippy were talking and listening to the music. Maybe I'd had enough to drink now, but I began to get irritated with the way the hippy was getting closer and closer to Susan. I leaned back in my chair, glanced under the table, and saw he was running his hand up and down her thigh. I looked up at her face and our eyes met. She smiled sweetly and moved closer to the guy.

"Hey," the hippy said, "you guys're great. Let's go somewhere else and party."

I moved my chair over, leaned around Susan, and saw that hand down there, creeping up between her legs. I reached around her, grabbed the guy's ponytail, and gave his head a sharp jerk.

"Hey, man, what's your problem? What's wrong?"

I saw he was surprised rather than angry, and I suddenly felt guilty for fucking with him.

"I'm sorry," he said, "Is this your old lady? No problem man, no problem. My mistake. Listen, you guys want another drink? I got some liquor at my house. We can go party or something, burn one down."

"Why don't you get us another drink?" Susan said.

The man stood up. "Sure, you got it. I'll be right back." He walked through the crowd to the bar.

"I'm really drunk," Pat said. "Those drinks are strong."

"Let's go," Susan said. "Now."

She and Pat stood up and walked to the exit. I was really drunk also and for some reason I picked up the heavy wooden chair I was sitting in and carried it out over my head, but no one said anything. Susan and Pat were in the lobby, laughing and drunk. The walls were lined with paintings from a faculty art show, some sort of boring, derivative, abstract expressionism.

"These paintings suck," Pat said.

"I like these two," Susan said, pointing out two lone impressionistic paintings.

I put down the chair and tried to take the two paintings off the wall. They were tied up with wire on clips. I had to really pull to get them off. I got them down, but I fucked them all up, someone's hard work. "Let's go," Susan said. "You're going to get in trouble."

We stumbled out to Pat's car. I tried to get the chair in the trunk but couldn't, so I threw it over into a big UT fountain along with the paintings. We all piled into the front seat, and I drove home. Halfway to El Madrid, Pat started throwing up. Susan held the back of her shirt while she puked out the window. By the time we reached the apartments, Pat felt better. She jumped out of the car and ran to the pool. Susan and I followed her to the pool's edge.

"Let's go swimming," Pat said.

"I'm gonna pass out," Susan said.

Pat started to take her clothes off.

Susan looked at me. "I'm going upstairs. Give me the keys."

Pat took off her underwear and jumped in the pool. "Come on in!" she yelled.

Susan walked up the three flights of stairs and didn't look back. It was cold, and the pool wasn't heated. I didn't feel like getting wet.

"Come on, Pat. You're gonna drown."

"No I'm not. Get in, you pussy!"

"C'mon, it's freezing. Let's go upstairs."

"Oh shit," Pat said.

"What's wrong?"

"I just ruined my watch. Help me out."

I pulled her out of the pool, and she put her arms around me, pressing her big wet breasts to my jacket.

"God, I'm cold. My dad's gonna kill me. He just bought me this watch for my birthday."

I helped her pick up her clothes. She tried to put on her

underwear but couldn't. I glanced up at the balcony and saw that several guys had come out to watch. Pat went up the stairs naked, holding her clothes in front of her. I followed close behind, watching her ass move. I thought: If Susan's passed out, I'm gonna fuck Pat on the couch.

Susan hadn't passed out, though. Pat and I walked through the door laughing and hanging on to each other. Susan handed Pat a towel and pajamas.

"I think I'm gonna be sick again," Pat said. She promptly ran into the bathroom and was.

"I'm gonna leave these pj's by the door, Pat. Are you okay?"

"Yeah."

"You can sleep on the couch. There's some sheets and a blanket."

"Okay."

Susan and I walked into the bedroom and lay on our mattress and box springs.

"That sure was nice of you to take care of Pat," Susan said.

"What do you mean?"

"I could just see your kindness. The way you stared at her all night."

"Why didn't you tell me that guy was touching your leg?"

"That guy was completely harmless."

"Why didn't you say anything?"

"You were guzzling those drinks."

"So were you."

"It was no big deal. I was handling it."

"Yeah, you were handling it."

"Maybe you want to go sleep with your cute little girl-friend Pat."

"I think I will."

I got up and went into the living room. I saw Pat leaning off the couch, throwing up into a pan, her wet hair hanging down around her face, and I went back to bed.

*　　*　　*

The buildings kept going up downtown, and Austin Paint and Spray kept painting them. I wanted to quit, but I needed money. Big Jim stayed on in 301 Congress, and Jesse and Tyler and I were moved to One American Center, the OAC, a big three-tiered building that looked like a tall ship, directly off South Congress, only a few blocks down from the giant Texas Capitol. The OAC was yet another building of so many going up that they were now starting to obscure and block the view of the State Capitol dome itself. Steve Hall was the foreman at OAC. Steve was a good guy to work for since he never wanted to work himself. He started whining at nine-thirty in the morning: "God, I don't wanna work today," or "I just feel like going home and going to sleep," or "They don't pay me enough for this shit."

Around eleven o'clock he'd want to go to lunch. "Come on, let's go to the Red Bean."

We went to the Red Bean then, ate some burgers, and got drunk. It soon became a routine. We were only supposed to take thirty minutes, but we took an hour and a half, sometimes two, and had many drinks, all on Steve. I came back so drunk some days I could barely hold a brush. Steve became very talkative and would follow me around the rest of the afternoon telling me about his five Yorkshire terriers or his sick mother, whom he was very close to.

"My dogs got into the garden again. My mother's in the hospital today. She's very ill. She's a very intelligent person, very funny."

He was a very depressed person. He always moped around wearing an old, blue Chicago Cubs cap and dark Ray-Bans whether he was inside or outside the building. He got smashed at lunch and went to the topless bars in the afternoon, spent all his money, and fell asleep by nine in front of his TV. He told me, "All I ever want to do is sleep." He'd practically beg me to go with him to the strip bars.

"Come on, man. Let's go to the Crazy Lady."

"I can't afford those watered-down drinks, Steve."

"That's okay, I'll pay for them."

"I don't know. You already bought everybody lunch."

"No problem, I got some money. I'll pay for everything."

"Okay."

So we went to the Crazy Lady after work. The bouncer at the door gave me a dirty long-sleeve shirt to wear over my T-shirt as this was a dignified establishment: No shirts without collars. We sat at a table, and sure enough, Steve started ordering drinks. Plain, unenthused girls danced on the stage to the horrible, generic rock, MTV crap that littered the eighties, Loverboy's "Working for the Weekend," the Outfield, or the latest pablum from Pat Benatar. We watched them jump around, and we drank. The prettiest one was a short blonde teenager with silver glitter on her tiny nipples. After she finished her dance, she came over to our table, sat next to me, and put her hand on my leg. She was very perky.

"Hi!" she yelled.

"Hi. You want a drink?"

"Sure, I'll have a vodka tonic."

"Steve?"

"Vodka tonic, coming up." He went to the bar and bought some more drinks.

"I liked your dance," I said.

"Thank you. I hope my mom and dad liked it."

"Huh?"

"They're sitting right over there. Hang on, I'm gonna ask 'em."

She hopped up and ran over to another table. An old couple sat there with beers in front of them. The woman had white hair piled up on her head, and the man had a crew cut. The girl talked with them for a minute and then came back over. I stared at her silver nipples.

"They loved it," she said. "Mom wants to know how much money I collect each dance. She said, 'Is that like a tip?' Where were you?"

"Huh?"

"Why didn't you come up?"

"I don't know."

"You want a lap dance?"

I looked over at her parents. "That's okay."

"Well, I have to dance again up there, then. Are you guys gonna come up and give me a tip?"

"Sure, we'll come up there."

"You better," she said and patted my leg and laughed. Steve brought the drinks, and the dancer picked hers up and walked backstage.

"Isn't this great?" Steve asked.

"Yeah, it's great." I gulped my drink down and watched the

next listless dancer. Steve started talking about some crappy TV show he loved called *Airwolf*, which starred a super helicopter and Jan Michael Vincent, in that order. Or he went on about a new show called *The A-Team*, starring George Peppard and a former bouncer turned bodyguard turned borderline actor with an afro Mohawk, named Mr. T. If it wasn't bad TV, again it was Steve's poor mother. "So now she's trying to get me to take care of her dogs, too, since she's so sick. She's the one who introduced me to Yorkshire terriers, actually. I said, No way, Mom, then I'll have *nine* Yorkshire terriers! Can you imagine that?" he asked me. "Nine Yorkshire terriers? Ready to breed?" He even started talking to the strippers of his dying mother and his Yorkshire terriers, and they pretended to care, shaking their asses and breasts up into his face, tapping their G-strings for dollar bills, which Steve continually filled, not for the titillation or a promise of future sex, but just to have someone to listen to him.

*   *   *

One day his mother did die. He'd told me so much about her I felt I knew her, too. He walked into an elevator lobby where I was painting a ceiling.

"Well, man, it finally happened."

"What's that, Steve?"

"She died yesterday."

"Who died?"

"My mother."

I stopped painting. "I'm sorry, Steve. That's terrible."

"She was really suffering. The cancer was eating her up inside. She'd been in severe pain for months, so she was heavily sedated when she died. I was there in the room with her last night."

"I'm sorry."

"She's gone."

"Do you have any other family?"

"No."

"You know, maybe you shouldn't have come in to work today."

"What else am I gonna do? This is it. You want to have lunch with me at the Red Bean? I'll pay."

"No, I'll pay."

"That's all right, let me pay."

"Okay."

"I'll come back up here at eleven."

He looked down at the ground and walked away, and I went back to painting my ceiling.

*   *   *

Tim Wilson, the big wheel at Austin Paint and Spray, was heavily involved in his small Holy Roller church and tried to be a father figure to all the guys. He had a local evangelical preacher who was also his friend who had started a half-ass church in a foreclosed two-story clapboard falling-down house he'd bought for nothing, not far from our paint shop in a shitty North Austin residential neighborhood. I knew him as Mr. Robertson, and he drove a long, four-door 1977 Lincoln Continental Town Car that was the same yellow color he dyed his hair. He always wore a shiny black suit with a wide red tie. Tim had several of his painters do free work for Mr. Robertson. Some had painted his large home, others had fixed up and painted the interior and exterior of the clapboard house Mr. Robertson had turned into a church, the inside all white, the outside lemon yellow.

One day Tim suddenly pulled me and another painter, a long-haired-loser-hillbilly-racist named Ricky, away from painting the One American Center building and had us follow him in his big white new Ford Econoline van to the yellow church, where Mr. Robertson was waiting, standing there in his suit, leaning against the gigantic Lincoln Continental, his arms crossed. I had started smoking small amounts of marijuana every morning before work to make it to lunch, and then took another hit off a joint after lunch to make it to 5:00 p.m. I had smoked weed for years, and it was easy for me to maintain. I wasn't getting totally wasted, just a couple of hits a day were enough to allow me to barely escape some of the mundane, repetitive reality of my job as a painter, so I always had a joint in my wallet now.

I didn't know Tim was taking us to his church, and I had just smoked a roach as we pulled up to Mr. Robertson. I was feeling paranoid when I got out of my battered LTD. Robertson was staring at me with disdain, but when the obviously-always-blasted, red-eyed Ricky got out of his old car, the yellow-haired preacher shook his head in disgust. He smiled, though, when Tim Wilson stepped out of the white van and shook his hand. Tim was hiking up his clean white pants on his fat ass, tucking in his white long-sleeve shirt, and talking rapidly. He seemed shy and nervous in front of his preacher, and it was interesting to see Tim in this new way, out of his element, out of the shop, kissing his preacher's butt. They spoke as though Ricky and I weren't there, and I listened and realized we were there because Mr. Robertson had installed a large concrete trough as a baptismal pool in the interior of his church, on the main stage, off to the side and behind his large cheap veneer pulpit. It looked like a long rectangular gray concrete hot tub he'd embedded into the stage with steps on both sides for his parishioners to walk down into in a line for him to dunk under the water and then walk up and out, like cattle being dipped for ticks.

Tim started ordering Ricky and me around, and we unloaded his van. I was disappointed to see it was full of several gallons, many cans, of A+B Blue poisonous epoxy. I was pissed that I didn't have a respirator on me either. Ricky and I would have to work quickly, and we did, mixing the epoxy paint resin together into five-gallon metal buckets, laying out long dropcloths carefully on the church stage. We climbed down inside the concrete baptismal trough and painted it from the top down with big four-inch brushes and rollers. Mr. Robertson was pissing me off also, standing over Ricky and me, watching our every move, ordering us around, repeatedly telling me to not get one drop of the blue paint on any pew or surface of his church. Thankfully the toxic fumes finally got to him, and he left us alone, speeding off and away in his yellow Lincoln.

Tim stayed, though, his first words to us as his pastor took off: "Hurry the fuck up, Ricky! Jake, I want this done already. I want this done now, immediately. This is costing me money." We did as told, rolled out the bottom of the concrete trough last so it would now all be sealed to be filled later with water that would appear clear and blue. We cleaned everything up, loaded the materials back into Tim's van, and got the hell out of there, Tim telling Ricky and me both to make it a quick drive-through fast-food lunch somewhere and to haul ass back down to OAC and get to work texturing and painting the miles of walls inside the multistory building.

*   *   *

Tim thought of himself as a good guy, and he probably did have a slightly above-average IQ. He loaned his workers, his men, money for personal problems (at 25 percent interest) or bailed them out of jail. He was convinced that most of his employees were trying to screw him out of money on their time cards, and most of us were. He had two gangly, messed-up teenage boys and all three of them fought regularly. We had to pull him off his oldest son one morning before he knocked the kid out. His temper flared often, and he put chairs through walls, overturned bookshelves, gave us no Christmas bonus, and then pouted out loud when no one in his company bought him a present. He had one answer to any money question you might have posed: "You're lucky you have a job," which in most cases was probably true.

One day Jesse decided to kick methadone, which was, he said, fucking up his life worse than it was already. He came into the shop that morning looking very ill. He always had that thick-skinned, yellow junky pallor anyway, but now it was worse. His face was almost green, he could barely keep his eyes open, and he slurred his words.

We were sitting in the smoke-filled shop reading the morning paper. I glanced at the classifieds for other jobs and found no hope there. I thought of Susan in her cubicle at the *Austin Times-Tribune*, sitting there on the phone all day, taking down every one of those ads, counting out every character to calculate each ad's cost. Tim Wilson had the front page, and he made a suggestion for solving the riot problems that were going on in South Africa at that time.

"What they should do is dig a big giant ditch and line all the niggers up in front of it. Then machine-gun them into the ditch, pour lime on them, and bury them."

Several guys laughed and agreed. Tim noticed Jesse propping himself up by the door.

"Jesse! What the fuck's wrong with you?"

"I told you, Tim. I'm trying to kick 'done. Don't you remember anything?"

"Shit, Jesse, you look like you're gonna die."

"I *am* dying. I can feel myself dying."

Everybody stared at him. A tape-and-floater said, "You look like shit, man."

"I feel like hammered shit."

"Maybe you better go walk around," Tim said.

"Okay."

Jesse limped out of the shop. I followed him into the parking lot. He leaned against a car and slowly slid to the ground. He pulled a bottle of pills out of his pocket and took three.

"What's that?"

"Percodan. It's what Justice Rehnquist takes, good stuff." He exhaled heavily. "I'm having trouble breathing. These things aren't worth a shit. I think I took about twenty of them yesterday."

"Give me a few."

"Fuck you, I need these. Here."

I held out my hand, and he shook five yellow pills into it.

I took one and put the rest into a piece of folded paper in my wallet.

"Jesse, you're green."

"This is ridiculous. What am I trying to do?"

"You need to go home."

"Fuck that. I need the money. I gotta work."

He put his head in his hands. The men started filing out of the shop, getting in their crappy cars to go to the job sites. Jesse had bought Susan and me dinner a few weeks before at the Hyde Park Bar and Grill. He'd been very funny and tried to pick up our Polish waitress by faking a Polish accent and saying he taught "retarded kids" crafts in Santa Fe.

"Thanks again for dinner the other night."

"My pleasure. You kids're great. I wish you success. I'm going to crawl under this car and die now. First I'm gonna drink the oil through the manifold."

Tim waddled out to us. His gut seemed to grow larger every month. When he reached us he dropped his pen and had to struggle to bend over and pick it up.

"Jesse," he said, "you need to go home."

"No, I can work."

"You're useless to me like this. Why did you even come in?"

"Because I need the work and I can do it, so just give me a place to go."

"Get out of here. You're pathetic."

"I'm trying to kick a powerful drug. Something you'd know nothing about."

"Listen, your drug problem's not my problem. I've put up with your drug bullshit long enough. Steve!"

Steve slowly shuffled up in his dark glasses and dirty Chicago Cubs cap. "Yeah?"

Tim pointed to me. "You guys go down to OAC. I want you to finish the seventeenth floor today. You've been down there for six fucking months, and you've only finished five floors."

"That's because you don't give me enough help."

"I don't want to hear any more bullshit excuses. You're fucking off and I know it. I've seen you guys walking around drunk on the streets. I want to see that job finished."

"I'm sick of this shit," Steve said. "I'm going to quit and you'll be fucked 'cuz you won't have one dependable foreman left since I'm the only stupid-son-of-a-bitch who doesn't sleep in closets half the day."

"So quit, goddammit!"

"Shit," Steve said and walked off toward his truck.

Tim turned back to Jesse. "Get the fuck out of here, Jesse. You're not dying in my parking lot."

Jesse slowly raised his head and tried to stand up. He fell down, and I helped him to his feet.

"Listen to me," Jesse began, "you stupid fat tub of shit. You talk about how religious you are, but you're a hypocrite."

Tim became incensed. "I got more religion in my little finger than you have in your entire body!"

"You wouldn't know God if he bit you on the ass."

"Get out of here! *Now*! Or I'll call the cops!"

Jesse stumbled over to his van. "That's okay, fine. I want to thank all my coworkers here for sticking up for me. I'll be back." He got in the van, started it, ran over the curb, and drove away, swerving all over the road.

Tim stared at me. "What the hell are you waiting for?"

"Nothing."

I got in my car and followed Steve to OAC.

*   *   *

A few days later Jesse did return. He was back on methadone and much improved. I was talking to him in the parking lot before he went into the shop. I don't know who called the police, probably Tim. Whoever it was, they suddenly drove up in force. Two blue-and-whites and one unmarked sedan.

Jesse and I stood very still. A chubby guy in a brown suit jumped out of the unmarked car, a gun in his hand, and ran toward both of us. Jesse looked at me and calmly said, "I guess I'm going back to jail."

The man in the suit looked very intense. He shoved me out of the way and threw Jesse against his van. All the painters and Tim came out of the shop. The man handcuffed Jesse, who yelled, "Thank you very much, Tim! I knew I could trust you! God loves you, man!"

I walked over to the shop. "What happened?" Steve asked.

"Jesse was wanted," Big Jim explained. "He's going back to the pen."

I asked him, "What for?"

Big Jim shrugged. "Something about fully automatic machine-guns, selling 'em."

They pushed Jesse into the car. I looked at the flashing lights and saw Jesse in the back seat talking to the policemen in the front seat. A cop walked up and talked to Tim.

"Go back in the shop," Tim said to us.

We followed his orders and went back inside the tin building.

*   *   *

Tyler, the banjo man, was another painter Tim now felt he'd carried too long. One morning Tyler came in ten minutes late. Tim started yelling at him, "You're gonna get docked, goddammit!"

"Listen, you fat bastard, I'm sick of your shit. I had some problems last night with Becky."

"You've always got problems with some woman. You've always got problems, period."

"You're a nosy bastard," Tyler said.

"And you're a drunk. I'm sick of covering for you."

"Fine, I'll quit and collect unemployment on your ass."

"The fuck you will, you won't collect shit. You're worthless, Tyler. You need to get your shit together and grow up."

"Listen, you ain't my daddy! I'm a man, goddammit! You don't tell me what to do. I got in a mean fight with Becky. I accidentally slapped her, and she left me for this guy with no nuts and I tried to kill myself, so there!"

"You're full of shit."

"Look, goddammit, that's why I'm late!" Tyler held out his arms. Both his wrists had tape and bandages on them. "You don't believe me? Look!" He ripped off one of the bandages and revealed two long red cuts with black stitches running vertically down his wrist.

"You've got psychological problems or something, Tyler, and I'm sorry about that. But you need to keep it at home," Tim said. "That shit doesn't belong up here."

"Fuck you. I don't know why I stay with you. Go ahead, fire me. I'll collect unemployment."

"I'm not gonna fire you yet, but you're gone for the day."

"Bullshit, I'm working today."

"You're going home."

"Well, shit, that's fine with me."

Tyler stormed out of the shop and slammed the door.

"Fucking retard," Tim said.

Everyone laughed a little and then started swapping mythical settlement yarns. I read my paper silently, in the corner, something about President Reagan opening up the state mental institutions and letting out the patients onto the streets, and calling them "homeless."

* * *

I made efforts not to associate with my fellow painters after work. It was bad enough seeing them forty hours a week. On Friday evenings everyone stayed up at the shop and drank for hours and talked, not wanting to go home, or having no home. I usually had a beer, bummed a cigarette, and left. I didn't want friends or any crap like that. But Tyler told me his problems more than anyone else, so I guess we were friends. His girlfriend, Becky, sparked yet another suicide attempt, and he went beyond work one afternoon and showed up at my apartment. Susan was spending the night with Norma, snorting crank and making crafts, bracelets and necklaces, well into the night, and so I was alone, sitting at our fold-out kitchen table, reading a book and eating a sandwich. I heard a weak knock.

"Come in."

Nothing happened. Another weak knock.

"Come in!"

Tyler walked in, and he had tears in his eyes. "Hey, man, I'm sorry I came by—"

"Hey, Tyler, what are you doing?"

"They got my dawg. They got Merle."

"Sit down. Who's 'they'?"

Tyler slowly sat down on my couch. He put his shaking head in his shaking hands. "They took Merle."

"Who took him?"

"I think it was that bitch Becky. I came home and he was off his chain. He ain't showed up yet."

"That's too bad."

"I've been in jail all night. Tim sent one of his boys down to bail me out. He said he's gonna fire me."

"Why were you in jail?"

"I'll tell ya. I went over to where Becky's been livin' since she moved out. She's livin' with this guy with no nuts, he's got this disease or somethin', an' so I went over there an' I was just talkin' with her out in the yard an' No-Nuts calls the cops an' they told me t' leave an' said I was drunk—"

"Were you?"

"Well, yeah. I had a bottle of whiskey in my coat. So, I left an' then I come back an' all I wanted to do was talk an' I felt I had a right to have at least one conversation, just an explanation. I told her she owed me half for three months of the electric bill an' that they was gonna cut it off. See, No-Nuts has some money an' she does too, an' all I told her I wanted was half and she said, 'Tyler, I'm callin' the cops,' an' so I said, 'Fuck it,' an' I just sat down on the curb and finished that bottle. Two cops came up an' they was a nigger an' a Mexican, an' the Mexican starts talkin' t' me like I was a little kid. He says, 'Dammit, Tyler, we're not gonna tell you again. You gotta leave this woman alone or you're goin' in.' An' I said, 'I'm a man, goddammit, the hell I'm goin' in.' So they handcuffed my ass, an' Becky starts cryin' an' sayin', 'I'm sorry, Tyler, I didn't want 'em to take you to jail,' and No-Nuts is out there with his bald leukemia head yellin' at me now, sayin' he's gonna press charges, an' I turned around t' him an' I said, 'Listen, Charlie, I'm comin' back over here tomorrow an' I'm gonna cut off your head, tie a rock around your feet, an' sink you in the Colorado River!' An' that nigger cop popped the shit outta me, hit me right in the face, hit me hard, an' he said, 'Don't you say one more word or I'll take the stick to your ass!' I can't remember anything else. I musta fought like hell last night. I got bruises all over me, an' there was five, big, black motherfuckers standin' there when they let me out this mornin'."

"Damn, Tyler."

"I get home, an' my worthless fuckin' cousin from Conroe is there. He's stayin' at my house, an' I really don't like that. He don't bathe, he stinks, don't clean up after himself, he won't do the dishes, he's always drunk. I told him he was gonna have t' leave. I don't wanna hear his sorry-ass problems, I got enough of my own. He better be gone when I get home . . . which is, uh, see, that's another thing: I don't have my truck no more."

"Uh-oh."

"An' you know Tim, if you ain't got a car, you ain't got a job."

"Where is it?"

"They impounded it, an' I can't get it out 'cuz I got all these fuckin' tickets. I was wonderin', uh, I knew you, uh . . . lived close by, maybe if you could give me a ride home. I know you're eatin' an all—"

"You want a sandwich?"

"No thanks, I'll just throw it up right now."

"I'll give you a ride home."

"Okay, man, I'd 'preciate it. I'm kinda in trouble right now."

"No problem, Tyler."

I finished my sandwich, locked the apartment, and we went down to the LTD. I'd put some windows in it now and propped them up with one-by-fours inside the doors. It was a vast improvement, no more rain or snow in the car, but it got hot in there since I couldn't roll them down. We drove around the corner to Tyler's duplex. I stopped in front, and Tyler got out.

"Oh shit," he said.

"What?"

"My cousin's still here."

"Well. . . ."

Tyler looked depressed. "Say . . . uh, you think I should call Becky? Just call her, maybe go by her house, just walk by—"

"I wouldn't go back over there, man. She's called the cops on you twice."

"I oughtta go bust out her windshield, like I did last time. Bust it out with her head."

"Listen, you really shouldn't go back over there. In fact, you should blow her off completely."

"You think so?"

"I know so. You need some time apart. I think if you stay away, maybe she'll call you."

"She's done that before. When I gave her the cold shoulder, she came crawlin'—"

"There you go. Just do something else. Maybe even get another girlfriend for a while—"

"But I love Becky. I wanna marry her."

I sighed. "Well, you can't marry her if you keep going to jail."

"I got other girlfriends, I guess."

"Call one of them, shit. If you go back to jail, you'll miss work and you'll be broke and fucked."

"Okay, man, thanks for the ride. Sorry 'bout bargin' in. Maybe . . . uh, you could . . . uh, give me a ride to work tomorrow or somethin' . . . . Maybe?"

I hesitated. "I don't think so. I have to take Susan to work every morning."

"Oh." He seemed upset. "Well, that's okay. I'll get up there some way. I guess I'll see ya tomorrow."

"Okay."

I went and got some gas, put some oil in the big leaky engine, and drove back to the apartment. I thought maybe I should give him a ride to work. But that was how it started. If I gave him one favor, he'd ask for a million more. I'd seen him mooch off everyone in the shop. I turned on the TV and forgot about it.

I got drunk that night and was late getting to work the next morning. I walked into the shop hungover and tired. I went into Tim's office. He was sitting behind his desk interviewing an old well-dressed painter. Some painters, the older they got (if they didn't disintegrate into nothingness) the more artistic they became, dressing like dandies almost, wearing funny hats, silly overalls, and sweaters. I handed Tim my time card so he could mark down my lateness. He checked everyone's punch-in time.

"You're late," he said loudly.

"I know. I'm sorry about that."

"You're late. You're ten minutes late."

"I said I'm sorry."

"It's seven forty. I'm gonna have to dock you thirty minutes for that."

"All right, Tim. What do you want me to do? Go back in time?"

"Huh?"

"It's already happened. I wasn't here and now I am. It's over, so quit telling me about it."

"I'm gonna have to dock you."

"Then dock me! Shit!"

Tim turned to the old painter: "What's his problem?"

I walked out of his office and into the coffee room. Everyone sat silently beneath a flickering fluorescent, reading their papers, smoke rising from their cigarettes and white Styrofoam coffee cups. I sat next to Jay, a congenial, muscle-bound country boy from San Marcos who was the best and highest-paid painter at APS. He asked me, "Did you watch the game last night?"

"No, I missed it."

I looked around the shop. It was the same every morning. We sat there like we were already dead, waiting for Tim to dole out some work. Some of us would go home, some would work. We never knew until the last minute.

"Hey, man," Jay said.

"What?"

"Did you hear about Tyler?"

"No, what?"

"He's in jail again."

"I just saw him yesterday right after he got out. I gave him a ride home."

"No, no, he's going to the big jail, Huntsville. He shot his cousin last night."

"No shit?"

"Shot him in the head."

"He killed him?"

"I think so."

Several others wearily lifted their heads and confirmed it. "Yeah. He killed him."

"Well, shit," I said. "Are they sure Tyler did it?"

"Yeah," Jay said. "He called the police and turned himself in. Tim was gonna fire him anyway."

"Yeah, he told me that."

Jay was looking at the sports section of the *Austin Times-Tribune*.

"Are you reading that?"

"Not really, here."

I began to read the front page of the paper, lit a cigarette, and waited for Tim to tell me where to work.

*   *   *

Susan and I moved out of the apartment. We wanted to get our own place since the apartments were so noisy. If creative people like Dwayne the filmmaker weren't dropping by, speed-freak couples were screaming and fighting with each other below us, or some guy was beating up his wife and kids next door, or somebody was stealing from somebody's apartment, or the guys next to us had their music turned up so loud the bass line shook my teeth.

We found a rent house in a nicer neighborhood called Harris Park. The house was very small, like a playhouse almost, just one room with a kitchen and half-bathroom, but it cost much more than the apartment, and the rent alone was tough to make. It was behind the garage of a nicer, normal-sized home rented out to a red-haired Episcopalian priest who was in school at the seminary across the street. He had a wife and two red-headed girls. Some cokehead girl from UT had lived in our shack before, and the place was full of roaches, giant clumps of them, moving in masses across the walls and floors. We roach-bombed it twice and barely made a dent in the population. I painted the tiny place, which was easy but our new landlord was very cheap and didn't reimburse me for my time or the paint or knock off any of the already exorbitant rent.

Susan was happy at first to be in the new Crackerjack box, and I guess I was too. The move broke us financially, but we had enough money left the first week to buy some food and dope and wine. We moved our stuff in, got drunk, and celebrated. I needed a raise to pay for our new high rent though, and a new transmission for the LTD, and on and on. I'd been at APS for a couple of years and still made only $7.50 an hour. I felt I did the same work as the ten-dollar-an-hour men now and wanted equal pay, but I had to catch Tim in a good mood, which was an incredibly difficult thing to do. I decided to hang around on a Friday evening. Everybody had been paid that day, and they were drinking and doping in the parking lot, figuring out ways to spend it all. Around six-thirty I told Tim, "I need to talk to you."

He look worried, said, "Oh shit," and walked away.

I cornered him in the shop. "I need to talk to you, Tim."

"So talk."

"In your office."

"I don't want to hear this shit."

"Come on. . . ."

Tim waddled into his office and eased himself down into the big leather chair behind his desk. "Are you gonna quit?"

"No, I want a raise."

"That's what I thought you'd say."

"Well, I need one."

Tim pulled out a file from a drawer—my file, I guess—and looked it over, tapping a pen on his desk. "You've been late a lot."

"I've been here about two years. I think I deserve a raise."

Tim stared at the file. "You know times are getting rough again. The commercial business has really slowed down. You're lucky you have a job."

I stared at him, his big jowls and shiny forehead. I sat there silently and waited for him to talk.

"Don't misunderstand me," he finally said. "We don't want to lose you. You're a good worker, you always have clean whites on, you show up for work, you have a car, you can talk to customers—"

"Then why can't I have a raise?"

"First I want to know what your intentions are."

"What?"

"What are your plans for the future? Are you just going to quit and run over to Mike at Mike's Interiors and use everything we've taught you over there? If you did that I'd be very disappointed."

I took a sip of my beer and spilled some down my shirt. "Tim, I don't know what my plans are. What I'd really like to do, if anything, is quit. I can't believe I'm even working here. I should probably go back to college."

He stared at me for a second and then shrugged. "Well, at least you're honest. Let me tell you something," he went on. "This wasn't exactly where I wanted to end up either, you know, babysitting a bunch of dumb-asses. When I was your age in Alabama I never knew I'd be running a painting business over here in shit-hole Texas trying to feed a family."

I leaned back in my chair. "Well, you're only forty."

"I'm thirty-nine. What I'm saying is I don't want to stay in this painting business forever either. Besides, the economy's slowing down. I'm seriously thinking about selling this business and starting a new line of work. A new profession. I've only told a few people about it."

"What profession?"

"You know I'm very active in the church."

"Right."

"You saw my pastor the other day—"

"He drives that yellow Lincoln."

"Right, that's him. He thinks I'm a real good public speaker. He let me give a couple guest sermons at the church. So, I don't know. . . . I was thinking of becoming a preacher."

"Really?"

I briefly saw that other side of him again. He seemed shy about it all, insecure. "Yeah. I don't know, maybe. What do you think?"

"I think you'd be a good one. I think you'd be perfect."

Tim smiled, his whole face brightened up. "Really? You think so? My wife thinks I can do it, too." He looked down at my file and pushed it aside. "Alright, I'll give you nine dollars an hour, but with more money comes more responsibility. I expect you to take some of that responsibility."

"Okay, I will. Thanks, Tim."

He opened the top drawer of his desk. "You coming to the Easter party?"

"I thought Easter was last week."

"No, it's this week. I'm having a party, and you better show up. You haven't come to one company party yet. You better be there."

"I will."

He pulled a vial out of the drawer, got up and locked the office door, and took a framed photo under glass of his family off the wall. "You can keep a secret, right?'

"You know it."

"You wanna do a couple lines? It's pretty good stuff."

"Sure."

Tim did out a couple of large lines. He handed me a rolled-up hundred-dollar bill, and I did half of a white line that stretched across the length of the picture. I swallowed and tasted the good bitter cocaine against the back of my quickly numbing throat. That first rush came, and I felt better than I had in months.

"Don't tell anybody I do this," Tim said, bending to the glass.

"No problem."

"Jesse was the only other guy who knew."

"And look what happened to him."

* * *

I was made a foreman then and hooked up with Jay, the friendly farm boy from a small town called Martindale, just outside of San Marcos, thirty minutes south of Austin. Jay and I would only paint residential now instead of commercial. It was strange when Jay and I painted someone's house; it was like we moved in with them for three or four weeks. Jay, with much more experience than me, set the tone for our behavior on the first job we did. It was a lawyer's expensive house in Tarrytown. After the man left in the morning, Jay opened his refrigerator, took out some milk and snacks, went into the living room, and turned on the big-screen TV. He even watched one of the guy's videos, some movie called *First Blood*, with Sly Stallone running around in the woods with a bandanna on his head shooting people.

Jay told me he was a real country boy, raised by a sorghum and corn farmer on their family land outside of San Marcos, where they worked from dawn until dark every day but Sunday. His father was now crippled by a stroke though, and in a wheelchair. Jay went to visit him often.

"He had the stroke, and then Mama had the tumor, they sold off almost all the land and now, he don't do nothing. He just sits in that goddamn wheelchair. I go out there every few weeks and take him out and drive him around. Last week I took him to see all the maize coming up. I pushed him down the road around the edge of the fields. I know he likes it, but he don't say nothing no more. His face is all paralyzed."

Jay's favorite subject was sports, particularly the high-school-football schedule of the San Marcos Rattlers. Every Monday he'd ask me: "Did you read about the Rattlers' game?"

"No."

"Oh, they're kicking ass, man. You gotta come out to one of the games with me. The Rattlers are gonna go all the way to state this year."

Jay said he had once been a San Marcos Rattler himself, had played football there, but was forced to drop out at sixteen when his girlfriend got pregnant. Now, on his second wife and several kids later, he still talked about his big mistake.

"I let my little head do the thinking for my big head. That bitch is taking me for everything now. She's married and has three of the kids and she's brainwashing them against me. I never should've fucked her, and now Sheila wants to have another baby. That's gonna be five. I can't even pay the support for the other ones, and this new dip-shit Attorney General Jim Mattox has that goddamn child-support law and they wanna throw my ass in jail or garner my wages. Man, I was a ballplayer, fastest guy in the school, faster even than the brothers, and then I shot it all to shit."

Jay had many, many problems, but he was always laughing and smiling about his fate, and I liked that. He was a religious man, a Christian like Tim Wilson, and went to church two times a week. But he had a secret wish he shared with me.

"I want to fuck a nigger whore. I just wanna do that one time before I die. See that big black ass in front of me and climb all over it. I'll never do it," he said sadly. "Sheila's gotta know where I am every goddamn second of the day."

While he talked, we painted and I nodded and said "Yes" and "Really" occasionally, but mostly I tried to let my mind wander. Leaning over somebody's toilet, painting their smelly baseboard, I'd daydream about being somewhere, anywhere, else. Whenever I did get there, Jay would walk into the bathroom and, however good-naturedly, bring me back home.

"Hey, man, you wanna go to San Marcos High tonight and kick some field goals with me?"

I got up from behind the toilet. "I'll pass, Jay."

"Come on, it'll be fun. Sheila's gonna bring a stopwatch and time me in the hundred. You'll get to see how fast this white boy really is. I'll prove I still got it."

"That's okay. I believe you."

"All right, man, you're missing out."

*　　*　　*

We were painting a big house that belonged to a successful insurance salesman named Mr. Abernathy. Jay was in love with the guy since he'd played football for UT years ago. Mr. Abernathy was also a very religious man and had sculpted praying hands jutting off the walls in every room. Church diplomas of some sort were framed and mounted. Bibles lay on the bedside tables next to pictures of his wife and daughters. When the family left in the mornings, Jay and I went through their papers and belongings as we did in every house, not trying to steal anything, just looking for something interesting.

Mr. Abernathy wasn't very tricky. I found two large stacks of *Cheri* and *Hustler* magazines hidden in his bathroom cabinets, their covers fairly tame, topless women with large bad perms. In just about every house I painted, the husband had some porn mags stashed somewhere. Jay and I went through them and put them back.

Later, though, I was painting the outside of the bathroom cabinets, and those magazines were staring me in the face. I took down one of Mr. Abernathy's *Hustler*s and shut the bathroom door. I looked at the magazine, found some nice shots of a long-haired brunette with a big round ass, and I stood in front of the mirror and masturbated slowly. After a few minutes, I came in their fake marble sink. I looked at myself there, in my painter's uniform, for several seconds. I wiped off then, put up the magazine, and started painting again.

*   *   *

I was working in a large custom home on Cat Mountain. The wealthy owner was an old tall German named Karl who followed us around all day watching every move we made. I was in a closet, on my knees, stoned, listlessly painting a baseboard. Karl came into the bedroom and started taking down the red curtains. He began to talk about the current administration and how much he admired it. When he praised our then–attorney general, Ed Meese, I couldn't stand it anymore.

"Ed Meese is a Nazi," I said.

"Young man," he said sternly and looked at me, narrowing his eyes. He was standing on a chair, the bloodred curtain draped over his arm. A lock of straight blond hair fell down over one of his eyes. He raised his chin, and the wrinkles disappeared from his neck. "You are talking to a former Nazi," he said proudly.

"Oh, uh, I'm sorry."

"I was forced to join if only to get a pair of pants. I was a member of the Hitler Youth, and there were many good things about the Youth that you won't see in your lying history books. Let me tell you, young man, Hitler made us feel good again. He gave Germany something to be proud about. All you know is what you have been taught in your little American schools with your little history books, which is to say, nothing. Hitler tried to make Germany great again and he almost succeeded, so the next time you say your words you should think about them and who you are saying them to."

I sat in the closet looking up at Karl on his chair. "Yessir," I said.

"Don't get any more paint on my carpet either. I see it everywhere."

"Yessir, I won't."

He strode out of the room, and I went back to painting the baseboard, carefully.

*   *   *

The Synott house was a large Tudor-style home in an older neighborhood. Mr. Synott, an emaciated stick of a man, worked all night at the 3M plant, while his wife, who conversely resembled a right tackle, worked nights at the Brackenridge Hospital downtown. During the day they watched us paint, sat at their kitchen table, and smoked. They smoked so much their ceilings were yellow and brown with tar. All the walls, cabinets, doors, and windows were covered in brown tar. Trash overflowed out of closets, sinks, under beds, over couches, and their eleven–year-old son seemed to run the house. He was fat and wore the same black pants and a dirty Pac-Man T-shirt every day. He ordered his mother or father to fix him a TV dinner and a Pepsi while he sat there transfixed by the television screen, playing video games. That's all I ever saw the family eat: TV dinners and Pepsis. They had an ancient woman they bullied around and kept holed up in a back room. She was the little boy's grandmother, the skinny husband's poor mother.

Every once in a while they'd let the old woman out, and she'd hobble around the house talking to me. There was something wrong with her back, and she had a huge gut she had to hold up with one hand like a sack of grain. She held a cane in her other hand. Her nose was a long fleshy knob that hung down over her mouth. She made a humming and snorting noise through it, and Jay and I could hear her coming from around corners. She'd ask her daughter-in-law over and over: "Diet Pepsi, please. Can I have a Pepsi? Diet Pepsi, please."

The daughter-in-law sat there and smoked and would yell at her husband. He was smoking and playing a video game with the boy on the floor. "Get her a glass of water, dammit! No Pepsi, Grandma!"

"Diet Pepsi, please."

"You can only have water and Fibersol right now."

"Oh thank you, a Pepsi please."

The grandma had a strong Swedish accent, which she explained to me one day.

"I'm from New Sweeny. Do you know New Sweeny?"

I was wiping tar off the den paneling with some toxic chemical. "No ma'am."

"It's out in the country, uh-hmmm, I'm Swedish, mostly Swedes, uh-hmmm, I had a farm but they rent it now, I had a farm, uh-hmmm, maybe a turkey dinner with mashed potatoes, hmmm? I used to work it. I built a wall, an' the inspector said, uh-hmmm, that's the best wall he ever seen, yes, hmmm. It don't go no more. Nice sweet family, my boy rents it, but it's my farm still, uh-hmmm, up in New Sweeny. You know New Sweeny?"

"No ma'am."

"I ain't seen it inna long time, no. They wanted me to build a road, county said, you gotta build a new road, an' I said okay, an' I built it. Cost me a lotta money, uh-hmm, yes, but I built it. I farmed there all my life. I helped build the walls, my boys help me. He used to fish, you like to fish?"

"Yes ma'am, I like to fish."

The daughter-in-law called out: "Granny, you leave those men alone!"

"Oh yes, uh-hmmm, oh yes, we gotta tank. We made that tank an' put fish in it. It don't go no more. My boy, he just like his daddy. My husband, you know, he was crazy. That's not right. He beat me."

"I'm sorry."

"Granny, leave the painters alone!"

"Uh-hmmm, he beat me all the time, yes. He broke my nose he did. Three times. He was crazy. I don't know what to do. I work so hard all the time, four children an' the farm an' the house an' the tank, an' he still beat me. An' he beat the children too, uh-hmmm, an' I told the church, an' I don't go to no church but they know 'cuz I told 'em, an' they took him away, an' you know, he died? Right later, uh-hmmm, he died. Something broke in his head."

The daughter-in-law came up and told Granny to go back to her room. "I told you to leave them alone."

"That's all right," I said.

"She's not bothering us," Jay said.

The woman insisted. "She has to go back."

"Okay, yes, uh-hmmm," Granny said. She started hobbling down the hall, trying to step over the trash. I let her hold on to my arm and helped her to the back of the house.

"It don't go no more. I'm sorry. I can't work no more. I work all my life. I run that farm all by myself an' raised the boys." She looked at me. I saw she had blue eyes deep down in her face. "I'm sorry, I work all my life. It don't go no more."

"It's all right, Granny."

I opened the door to her back room. A strong fecal smell hit me in the face. There was no light. A small plastic toilet on wheels sat in the middle of the room surrounded by wads of stained toilet paper. The carpet was littered with trash, TV dinners, cans of Fibersol. As I helped the old woman to her bed I noticed quite a few beer cans piled near her headboard.

"You like to have a beer every now and then?"

"Oh yes, uh-hmmm, my grandson will give me one, a Diet Pepsi. I'm sorry, it don't go no more. Will you paint my room?"

"We'll paint it tomorrow."

She turned her head to the wall. I stepped over the trash and shut the door quietly behind me. I walked out of the house and to the LTD at the street. I left my paintbrushes there, my little tool bag full of putty knives and mud blades. I didn't even say good-bye to Jay.

*   *   *

I figured Susan would be pissed that I quit my job, but as it turned out, she wanted to quit her job also, and it was sort of my fault. I knew she hated selling classifieds at the paper and was miserable there. I was the one who had been encouraging her to use her family connections through her mother or her uncle Martin to maybe try to get a job in the film business. If not as an actress, I figured they could at least get her on a crew, a real paying job on a real movie, as the business was just starting to take off in Austin. I suggested she ask Betty Sue to ask Martin, and eventually, apparently, she had. I shouldn't have been surprised or pissed but I was both, especially when she told me she could get on a show but she was not going to get paid after all, that she was quitting the *Austin Times-Tribune* to work as an intern on a pilot for a TV series that Martin had written for CBS.

I shook my head. "Susan, you can't work for free. This sounds like Dwayne Coleridge and his crappy art-house-indie-movie bullshit."

"No," she said, adamant. "That is not it at all. This is how you get into the real film business. Martin works on real movies, or, mostly real TV, but he said television sometimes pays even better. And if you can get just one movie, just one TV show on your résumé, then you're in and start getting paid, maybe even on the same movie, halfway into it, if they see you working, if you make yourself indispensable."

"Yeah, but we can't even get a decent car or pay the rent for this little playhouse. How the hell can we afford for you to be an intern on some TV show?"

"Well . . ." she hesitated, "you know my mom was staying in Martin's backhouse but she's moving back to Cypress. Martin just said we could move in there now though, for a while. He's got this cute little cottage behind his house, and he said we could stay there for free."

"I am *not* gonna sponge off that guy."

Her mouth tightened. "It's not *sponging*," she said, and then her voice softened. "Besides, he likes you, Jake. Martin likes you. He gave you all of those nice jackets of his, that camel hair coat."

"They didn't fit."

"Maybe he could even help you get an agent or something. In fact I *know* he could help you get an agent."

"I don't need his help."

"I know you don't, but it's just . . . he's a real writer like my dad was and—"

"So I'm not a real writer now?"

"Come on, you know that's not what I meant. You know I love your stuff. But seriously, he's rich. He's a well-published screenwriter *and* a producer. He's connected. He could really help you. He could help *both* of us. Okay?" She sounded a little desperate. "He has that beautiful house in Westlake, and my mother already works for him." She looked around our little roach-filled one-room efficiency cabin. "We could get out of this fucking place."

I glanced about the room. It was better than the El Madrid apartment but still pretty grim, and even smaller. I thought about it, all of it, long and hard. I lit a cigarette.

"I don't think so." This was the wrong answer, and I could see she was getting pissed, which just made me angry also. "I think I'm gonna hit the road. And listen, I'm gonna take the LTD. I'm sure your *mother,* or that *real* writer 'Uncle Martin,' can help you get around now, if you wanna go live with him."

"Fine," she said. "You can have that piece-of-shit car."

I packed a little canvas laundry bag, right then, and Susan started crying, and I drove away. My grand gesture didn't get me very far, though. The odometer, and many other things, had stopped working years ago on the '72 LTD. The two-door behemoth had a 400 V-8 in it that drank and leaked so much oil I didn't even bother to change it anymore. The black fluid poured out from beneath the car as I drove. Whenever I parked, so much oil dripped out that I had to put a fresh piece of cardboard under the engine at almost every house I'd ever painted so as not to soil the street or driveway in front of any customer's home. I always kept at least two cans of 10W-30 motor oil in the backseat and would pour one in regularly, pulling the dipstick and checking it every other day I drove that car. I must have forgotten to pour in a can though, here or there—two or three cans—something happened. I made it only ten miles, just above North Austin off the Highway 360 loop, before the LTD threw a rod and finally died.

HALLOWEEN

There were many fly-by-night, one- or two-man businesses on the outer edges of cities in Texas that often sprang up along the main freeways, I-10 cutting through San Antonio from east to west, or the I-35 corridor running into Austin from south to north. Most of these men sold raw materials from the surrounding countryside or articles shipped in cheap on trucks from Mexico. There were flagstone businesses that were nothing other than a dozen large piles of carefully stacked white and yellow limestone not twenty yards off the freeway access road with a handpainted sign on a four-by-eight-foot piece of plywood that read "Mike's Rocks." Most of them also had at least one small construction trailer or a mobile home along with whatever their material was—say, ten large conical piles of dark-brown soil next to a dump truck, one small bulldozer, and another sign, "Bert's Dirts."

Some only had a large tent as an "office," and they were surrounded by dozens of poorly executed wooden chainsaw sculptures of bears, eagles, and other animals carved quickly out of large logs of cedar or cypress. Or someone had cut dozens of leaning-cowboy silhouettes, large lone stars, or the shape of the state of Texas out of steel with a blowtorch and painted them black or red, white, and blue, and they were selling them, right next to another business of concrete lawn figures and fountains and a metal prefab building that had a crew of undocumented Mexican workers in it, cranking them out of a concrete mixer and molds with one white guy ordering them around who had hired them all for peanuts. The businesses that had at least graduated to a building, whether sheet metal or wooden, sometimes became more established and stuck around, but most of these operations tore themselves down, packed up, and disappeared as fast as they had arrived.

This business was called Danny's Grass and Wood. It was in the northern part of Austin, off the 360 Loop, past 183. It consisted primarily of a few large hills of unstacked cut live-oak firewood and two, long, parallel rows of St. Augustine grass on pallets, with a new white construction trailer out front, right off the freeway, and a smaller, dingy mobile home behind it. The proprietor's name was—Danny. He was about forty-two, forty-three, and, he told me, an official born-again Christian.

"You get a lot more business being born-again," Danny said. "I've been looking through the Christian yellow pages, and there's this whole network of Christian businesses you can hook up with."

We sat in his office, the little trailer off the freeway. Danny told me about his life while we smoked a joint. He'd been a welder for most of it in South Texas. Ten years before, he smuggled dope in trucks into New Mexico. "I got into a fight one day in Santa Rosa with a bunch of Indians. One of them took a

brick and knocked my whole jaw off. See, I've had reconstruc-
tive surgery. They had to rebuild my entire jaw. These aren't
my real teeth either." He turned his head and showed me where
they'd stitched him together. I could see the pink scars. His face
had a plastic, rubbery shine to it and moved in the wrong directions whenever he talked. "They took a bunch of skin off of the
back of my legs and used it on my face," he said.

He took me behind his office and showed me the old mobile
home. "You can stay in here." We went inside. It was a one-
room place with a cot, a hotplate, a card table, and a fold-out
chair. A tiny old TV with a long antenna sat on top of a crate
in a corner. The whole place smelled like beer vomit. "I'll pay
you five-fifty an hour."

* * *

It was October. Danny said he usually sold St. Augustine grass
and firewood, but he was going to try pumpkins for Halloween. A truck and trailer pulled in one day and backed up to the
yard. Danny had just hired another worker named Vicente. He
was young, from Guatemala, and spoke no English.

"He lives somewhere around the corner, I think," Danny
said to me. "It's great 'cuz he can walk to work. The cash I give
him is a lot of money in his country."

We worked all day on unloading the pumpkins. There
were many rotten ones that broke and reeked. Once we were
through, Vicente had to go around and pick up all the rotten
pumpkins, throw the orange-and-black goop into a wheelbarrow, and dump it in the backyard. Danny said he had a special
job for me.

"I want you to go down to Smithville Grass and Wood."

"Who's that?"

"They're my main competitors, and they're bastards. Everything they sell is at the lowest possible price. They're just a bunch of cedar choppers, and they'll act like they're dumb, but don't let the old man trick you. He's a tough businessman. I want you to go down there and tell him you want to buy a pumpkin and get their prices. Be real casual."

I got in one of the two flatbed trucks Danny owned and drove up 183 to Smithville Grass and Wood. It was definitely a more permanent, storelike operation, with a long metal three-sided warehouse behind it filled with all their stacked firewood and green grass ready to go on pallets. They even had a large wooden one-story cabin up front that served as an office and some sort of general store that sold mostly red-white-and-blue caps, T-shirts, more leaning metal cowboys and lone stars, the standard cheap Texana bullshit. They also already had many neatly stacked piles of pumpkins for sale. A skinny old hillbilly, Mr. Smithville, came out smiling and greeted me personally. He showed me his pumpkins proudly. I asked a few questions as if ready to buy but then said I had to bring my kids back to pick out the pumpkins they wanted. The smile dropped off his face. He thanked me and walked away. I drove back to Danny's Grass and Wood.

"He's charging fifteen cents a pound."

"Fifteen cents!? Are you sure? Are you sure you didn't get it wrong?"

"Yeah, I'm sure. Fifteen cents."

"Well, shit. I can't charge that low. Go check out the prices at the Tom Thumb grocery."

I got back in the truck, drove to the store, found out the prices, and came back.

"Thirteen cents a pound."

"Son-of-a-bitch! Are you sure?" He looked at me suspiciously. "Are you sure you're not wrong? Huh?"

"No, I'm not wrong."

"I can't beat that. I'm gonna have to charge twenty cents to make a decent profit. What do you think of that? You think that's good?"

"You're asking me?"

"Yeah, I'm asking you. How much do you think we should charge?"

"Less than twenty cents a pound."

"How much less?"

"Shit, I don't know. They're your pumpkins."

"That's right. I guess I'll charge eighteen cents a pound. That sound good to you?"

"Sure."

We went into the trailer, and Danny showed me the scale to weigh pumpkins on.

"This scale cost twenty-five dollars so be careful with it. Keep an eye on it. Don't let anybody steal it."

"Okay."

"Be careful with it when you weigh those big pumpkins. If you break it, you have to buy me a new one."

"Okay."

He gave me another tour of the grounds, and we smoked a joint. He had some ugly patio furniture for sale and asked me to memorize all the prices. There were also several large heavy barbecue-pit smokers. All were very expensive. Danny wanted me to memorize a little speech he'd made up to tell customers about the smokers, but he couldn't remember it himself. He gave me a little booklet on their construction instead. We walked back through the yard, went over the grass prices one more time. All the St. Augustine was stacked on pallets, and it was turning yellow and brown. He saw me looking at it.

"It just does that," he said. "It turns green again when you plant it."

"Right."

Vicente was out there working, stacking a small supply of oak logs and throwing away rotten pumpkins.

Danny drove away. Whenever he left, I was supposed to sit at the phone and wait for pumpkin, grass, firewood, patio furniture, or barbecue-pit customers. I spent most of my time smoking his dope. Danny had said I could help myself to the large bag of "Mexican shit weed" in his desk anytime, so I did. One day, at his request, I made a flimsy scarecrow out of old clothes and hay Danny had left me and put it next to a stack of pumpkins by the freeway. It was supposed to attract customers, he said. Few came, and nobody called.

Danny was gone a lot. One day he happened to return just as a woman was driving up in a station wagon. She and several kids jumped out. The kids ran around the pumpkins Vicente and I had stacked up around some scraggly trees next to the highway. They looked at my scarecrow. The woman asked me if we had any pumpkins for sale.

"Yes ma'am."

"How much are they a pound?"

Danny stepped between us. "Well," he said. "The big ones

are eighteen cents and the little ones are twenty-five cents a pound. They're more expensive."

"They're only thirteen cents a pound at Tom Thumb for all sizes," the woman said.

Danny looked at me and frowned.

"Uh, yeah," he said, "but, uh, these are organically grown."

"They are?"

"Yeah, up in Deaf Smith County. They got lotsa organic stuff up there."

"Oh well," the woman said. "I was hoping I could maybe buy a few big ones and you'd give me a bag of those little ones for the kids."

"I don't know about that," Danny said.

The woman was very nice and polite. "I'm sorry, it's just that they're from the orphanage." She smiled. "I work at the orphanage off Highway One and we don't have a budget to speak of. I have enough money for a few of the big ones, but I can't pay for all the little ones. See, we were hoping every child could have his own little pumpkin. We're having a Halloween party."

"Well, I'm sorry about this," Danny said. "But I can't just give them away."

"I can probably bring some more business down here," she said. "I know some other teachers who need pumpkins for their classes."

Danny looked at me and the woman warily, as if we were in it together. "Listen, I'm sorry, but how do I know that's true? Those teachers could come down here and ask me to give 'em away too."

"I guess they could," the woman said. "Come on, kids."

The children were confused. "No pumpkins? We can't get any pumpkins?"

"No, the prices are too high here. We'll go down to Tom Thumb."

"I can't give 'em away," Danny said.

The woman said nothing, loaded up the kids, and drove off.

"Shit," Danny said, "that was our first customer."

*　*　*

Not many people were buying Danny's pumpkins. As Halloween approached, they rotted in increasing numbers. Vicente hauled them off, working hard all day. I sat in the trailer. Every once in a while I'd sell a pumpkin, or Danny would send me off in a rickety truck, pulling a rickety trailer, overloaded with St. Augustine pallets to deliver to someone's yard.

My first delivery was a large one in a new subdivision off MoPac, unloading three full pallets of grass onto some doctor's bare dirt front yard to give him a lawn. When we were finished, he and Vicente and I stood back at the edge of the street and surveyed all our hard work. The grass was obviously dying when seen as a large yellow and browning whole, with only a few hints of rectangular green here and there. The doctor shook his head.

"It just does that," I said. "It turns green again when you plant it."

He stared angrily and reluctantly handed me a check made out to Danny. We got in the truck and got the hell out of there. I couldn't blame him. I didn't believe it either.

*　*　*

When Vicente rode in the truck with me, we'd try to talk. I spoke a little Spanish from a semester in college and growing up in Central Texas. The first thing that Vicente got me to understand was that he wanted some clothes. I told Danny about it.

"He wants to go to the store."

"He wants everything. He smells like shit. I told him to take a bath."

"It's his clothes. They have rotten pumpkins all over them."

"Tell him to change his fucking pants."

"Those are the only ones he's got."

"Well, shit. All right, I'll take him to Kmart. Answer the phones."

He drove away with Vicente and left me in front of the silent phones.

Halloween came and went. In spite of my scarecrow and lowering prices to seventeen cents a pound, Danny sold few pumpkins. Almost all of them had rotted anyway, and Vicente hauled them off.

*   *   *

Danny came in one day wearing a new, expensive, Western-style suit and new cowboy boots and a white hat. "I'm thinking of running for sheriff," he explained.

Another day he bought an unusually expensive speaker phone for the office trailer. He couldn't figure out the buttons, and nobody called anyway. Then he ran off and dropped a bunch of money on two mobile phones for his trucks that barely ran. The mobile phones were from Motorola, two large beige plastic bricks with black antennas. The one for the truck had to be attached to some battery bag to keep it charged. They cost about fifty cents a minute to talk on, but Danny was very excited.

"You can reach me from all over the city. I can call in wood orders to you while you're still out delivering."

"Great."

The mobile phones didn't work at all. It seemed they had a range of about five miles or so and hung up on the caller constantly. They worked correctly one time when I had to call Danny and tell him the police had just pulled me over and given me four tickets personally because of his piece-of-shit truck, and that they were questioning Vicente about being an illegal immigrant.

"Did you tell them my name?" he asked me.

"It's on the side of your truck."

"Oh yeah. But not my last name. Just get out of there."

I hung up, gave them Danny's last name, his address, everything, and they let me go. But they kept Vicente, yanked him out of the truck, stuck him in their car, and sent him back to Guatemala.

* * *

Nobody bought any of the crap he had lying around. People stopped by occasionally out of curiosity, saw the high-priced patio furniture, the expensive barbecue smokers that weighed several tons apiece, rotten pumpkins everywhere, and they drove away. The grass business was down because it was fall and the economy was down, and when the economy's down, I guess the last thing people need to do is run out and sod their yard. I sat in the trailer with Danny, smoking dope, and it drove him crazy that he was paying me and there wasn't much to do.

His driver came in one day, delivering a full load of brown St. Augustine pallets to the yard. The driver's name was Pete, and he talked to me while Danny looked over the truck. Pete told me he was pissed because Danny rarely paid him, and when he did the checks bounced half the time. The big semi he drove constantly broke down, and it was Danny's truck, not Pete's, and he felt Danny should have to fix it rather than blame him for everything that broke. Pete then told Danny this, and Danny threatened to fire Pete on the spot.

"You don't know how to drive a truck, goddammit! I oughtta can your ass right now. What did you break this time?"

Pete was nervous and stammering. "Don't fire me, Danny. I need this check to pay my electric and water. I gotta lotta bills, an' child support an'—"

"I oughtta take this shit outta your check. What did you say was broken?"

"Uh, it's that spring under there. I told you we loaded too heavy this time."

"Well, Pete, we gotta overload because if I don't overload I don't make any money, and every other driver I've ever had who's overloaded don't get pulled over or break down near as much as you."

"I'm sorry, Danny. I'm just doing what you tell me. I know I told you 'bout that leaf spring before. I thought it was gonna break."

"Yeah, yeah. . . ." He looked at me. "Go get that big wrench up in the cab."

I ran up to the cab, climbed in.

"It's under the seat!"

I found the wrench and ran back. "Come here," Danny said and crawled under the flatbed.

I crawled under there in the mud and we looked at the leaf springs. They were five-inch-wide strips of half-inch steel stacked together. The top strip was clearly broken into two pieces. A large nut and bolt held all the strips down.

"See where it's cracked?" Danny asked.

"Yeah."

"Let's take that bolt out and look at that top one."

I put the wrench on the nut and started to turn. It never occurred to me that the truck was still overloaded and that a thousand pounds of pressure were on those leaf springs and that the nut was the only thing holding it back. I put my body and head directly above it and started to turn harder. It wouldn't budge.

"Turn it," Danny said.

I leaned away from the springs and pulled on the wrench with all my weight. There was a loud clang and pop, and several large pieces of steel exploded upward. I was dizzy for a few seconds and didn't know what had happened. I heard Danny's voice faintly: "Oh my God. Oh shit."

I looked down at my right hand. My index finger and my middle finger were broken and twisted out at odd angles. All the skin was scraped off the top of my hand and half my thumb was missing. A red stream of blood spurted forcefully out of the hole. I held my right hand up with my left hand and crawled out from under the flatbed. Pete helped me over to another truck.

"Shit, this hurts," I said.

Danny ran around panicking. "Well shit! Just take it easy, everybody just take it easy, all right? You're all right. You still got your fingers. Goddammit! Where's the emergency room? Where's the hospital?"

"There's a minor emergency center up the road," Pete said.

"Okay, shit, let's go," Danny said and jumped into the truck. Pete handed me a dirty rag. I put it on my right hand and got into the truck. Danny talked to me as we sped down the freeway.

"You're going to be all right. Are you okay? You're turning pale. Are you okay?"

I could barely hear him. Everything started turning white, from the outside in. I heard a loud steady buzzing sound in my ears.

"I think I'm passing out."

"Don't worry, man. I'll get you to a hospital."

We drove to a little strip mall, and Danny got out and ran inside what looked like a medical office. I stepped out of the truck, and my blood ran down my arm and dripped on the sidewalk. Danny ran out of the office.

"Get back in the truck. Hurry up. You're bleeding all over the place."

"What about the doctor?"

"This is a dentist's office."

I climbed back in the truck, and we eventually found the emergency center. Danny took me in, talked to a nurse, and said to me, "Are you gonna be all right? I have to go back to the trailer. Nobody's at the phones."

"I'll be fine."

"Don't worry, I told 'em I'd pay for it."

"Okay."

He left. The nurse X-rayed me and cleaned the oil and dirt out of my torn skin. She scrubbed hard and fast. "I know this hurts," she said. "But I have to do it."

I told her it was okay, and the doctor came in.

"Your wrist is broken," he said. "These two fingers are broken, too."

He straightened out my fingers, taped them up, sewed up my half thumb, bandaged my hand, and put a cast over my wrist, and I called Danny. The doctor prescribed some codeine painkillers, and when Danny arrived I asked him to take me to the pharmacy. He seemed pissed.

"What for?"

"I need these pills."

"I suppose you want me to pay for them. . . ."

He paid for them and we went back to Danny's Grass and Wood. I went to my little trailer, and Danny followed me in. I found a warm beer under the card table, took the lid off the pill bottle with my teeth, and downed several of the pills.

"Do you really need those?" Danny asked.

"Yeah, I do."

"Give me a couple."

I poured two out on the card table, and Danny swallowed them dry.

"Are you sure you really broke your wrist?" he said. "I thought I heard the nurse say it wasn't broken. They didn't cast your whole arm"

"They cast halfway up it," I said.

"You know," he said, "when I was working as a rough-neck out in West Texas and something like this happened, they would've just slapped a bandage on it and told me to go back to work."

I sat down on my cot and had another swallow of beer. "Oh yeah?"

"Yeah."

Danny stood there for a minute, his hands on his hips. "So, you're just gonna lay here now?"

"Yep."

"You can't sue me, you know."

"I wasn't planning on it."

"Good. That's good."

I didn't say anything else, and he finally left.

*   *   *

It started to get a little colder after that, and some wood orders trickled in. I took the orders, found the different routes to the houses on the city map, and tried to write down the directions for Danny with my left hand. He had to deliver the orders now, but he kept asking me when my hand would get better.

Every couple of days he sent me down the road with a check and a flatbed, and I bought several cords of wood from another business off 183. The owner's name was Greg, and he was short, and fat, and had a little black mustache. He was always talking to me, telling me what a great hunter he was. Every time I went there, he had another little pink deer hanging up by its legs under a tree, all of its skin ripped off, dripping blood, and covered in flies.

Greg had a little firewood factory going with twelve laborers working on an assembly line from six in the morning until dark, seven days a week. They stacked wood on a conveyor belt in small bundles, wrapped them in plastic, put them on pallets, and stacked them in a warehouse. I pulled up to their large, loose woodpiles, and they loaded four cords onto the flatbed. I'd get out and help them stack the wood with my left hand. The workers complained to me in Spanish. Basically they said that they hated Greg and that he wasn't paying them enough money. After we loaded the truck, I drove it back to Danny's and slowly restacked the wood in his yard. Danny watched me stacking wood one-handed for a week or so and followed me around, asking questions.

"So how's your hand feel? You gonna be ready to deliver soon? You still got part of your thumb. You know, if you lose your thumb, sometimes they'll sew your big toe on there. You need a thumb more than you need a big toe. Can you go out there yet? You think you're ready?"

"I should get the cast off in a couple weeks," I said.

He looked pissed.

"All right, fine, I'm paying you to sit around all day and stack wood, but that's okay, I guess that's okay! Fuck it!"

He walked into the office trailer, and I kept stacking.

Business was bad. Danny said he was losing money by the handful. A cold front had come through, but it was a weak one and people weren't ordering firewood. One day a young husband and wife pulled up on the side of the road in an old truck. They set up a few stacks of wood and a sign they'd painted in big red letters that said "Firewood for Sale." They had a sloppy Christian fish symbol painted under the letters, dripping red.

"Go see what those people are doing," Danny said.

I walked over there and talked to them. They both wore old jean jackets, and their faces were sunburned and thin from hunger. The woman was tall, with unusually long blonde hair she'd put into a thick braid that ran down her back like a tail. They said they only had a little bit of wood to sell. They'd cut it off the land they were living on. Their little boy was with them. He had snot and dirt all over his face and was bundled up in a cheap coat, standing by the road with cars whipping past. I went back and told Danny what was up.

"I don't like it," he said. He walked over to the edge of the highway, talked to them for a minute, and came back.

"I told them to leave," he said, "but then they told me they were born-again Christians too, so . . . you know, I guess they can try it out. There wood's shitty anyway, an' those little stacks they sell are expensive. They're not gonna make any money. People get a much better deal buying a full cord from me."

"Right."

"Did you see that guy's wife? That hair goes down past her butt."

"Yeah."

"I told her I had a little boy too, an' she started talking to me. Kids are great conversation starters. She's a good-lookin' lady."

"Oh yeah?"

"Maybe her husband will leave and she'll come over to the trailer. I'd like to bend her over a chair, grab that ponytail, and fuck the shit out of her. I bet she really likes to fuck. She smokes. A girl that smokes likes to fuck. Maybe I can get her to come give me a blow job or sit on my lap."

"Maybe."

Nobody fucked him, but later that day the Christian couple did sell some wood. They were down the road about twenty yards from Danny's sign. People stopped by their truck often and bought small bundles of wood. The next day they had even more customers. Danny called me into the trailer from stacking wood.

"Run 'em off," he said.

"Who?"

"Who do you think?" He pointed to the couple at the road. "They're taking away my business."

"Okay."

"Maybe I should sell little bundles of wood instead of these big cords. What do you think?"

"Man, I don't know."

"The math calculations I made on this wood will be all screwed up, though. . . ." He sat and thought. "I don't know. Maybe I *will* sell little stacks . . . maybe—" The phone rang and we both jumped. "Go ahead and get rid of them." He answered the phone: "Danny's Grass and Wood."

I walked back out to the couple on the side of the road. I talked to them for a while. The little boy was standing up in their truck bed now, staring at me. I saw the truck was old and falling apart. I asked them how business was.

"It's going great," the husband said. "This is a good location."

"Yeah," I said, "that's what I wanted to talk to you about. See, well, Danny said that a policeman stopped by here yesterday evening and told him there's a law against people selling things this close to the road. It's some county ordinance or something, but the police told Danny y'all need to move."

"We gotta leave?' the husband asked.

"Yeah, but the county ends about a mile or so from here. If you just move down the road a ways, it'd probably be all right."

"Does he want us to move right now?"

"Yeah, I guess so."

"Can we have a minute to load up?"

"Yeah, sure."

"We made a lot of money here yesterday," the wife said.

"You got some good wood."

"We both cut it together," the wife said.

I stood there. "Yep, it's good wood. . . . Well, I gotta go back to work."

The husband told his son to get out and started loading up the truck bed. He nodded his head to me sincerely. "Thanks."

"All right."

I walked over to the trailer and went inside.

"Well?" Danny said.

"They're going up the road."

"I hope they park in front of Smithville Grass and Wood. He's trying to sell all that crappy wood. Okay, good, now go out there an' load up the white truck with small pieces of wood. Pull it out there next to the highway and make a bunch of stacks of wood where they were."

"Okay."

"And put up a sign that says 'Firewood for Sale.' And put a fish on it. How much were they charging again?"

"Fifteen bucks."

"Let's charge twenty."

"Okay."

"Get them as close to the road as you can."

"Okay."

"Have you eaten lunch yet?'

"No."

"Let's just skip lunch today."

"All right." I started to leave the trailer and stopped. "Hey, I just remembered. Yesterday was payday."

"Was it?'

"Yeah, what happened?"

"Well, I forgot. Can't people forget things?'

"Yeah, but not my check."

"Listen, can I pay you tomorrow?"

"I kinda need that money."

"I gotta make some deposits. If you wait one more day it sure would help me out. I don't want to have to write you another hot check."

"All right."

I walked out of the trailer. Danny yelled after me: "Make those stacks three feet high!"

* * *

The weather turned warm again. It was November and eighty-eight degrees. Nobody bought the stacks of wood. Danny said he had another idea: used cars. He started leasing out the highway frontage to a salesman who said his name was Johnny Florida. Johnny had a large potbelly, long sideburns, and always wore huge mirrored sunglasses. Every day he wore the same brown slacks, a pink shirt, and a red-and-black Windbreaker that said, "Red Adair Oil Well Firefighters" on the back. He drove a blue Trans-Am and wore a scraggly toupee that moved up off his scalp whenever the wind blew. The first day I met him, he was underneath the dashboard of an Impala turning back the odometer. He continued to reset the odometers on every car he had, and put the vehicles out by the highway where my little firewood stacks had been. Then he hired an unemployed electrician to sit inside Danny's office trailer and wait for customers.

The electrician brought a couple of joints to work every day, and we smoked them in the trailer while Johnny and Danny rode around in Johnny's Trans-Am talking about how much money they were going to make. After about two weeks Johnny sold one car, and he and Danny immediately started arguing. Johnny was supposed to give him a commission on each sale, and now he didn't want to cough it up. Danny got pissed and yelled about Johnny's girlfriend calling the trailer all day and about how he'd advanced Johnny the first lease payment on the lot. He also said something about blowing Johnny's head off. Johnny became nervous and paid him.

Shortly afterward he made another sale. I was the only one on the lot. The electrician was gone. Johnny had never paid him, so he quit. Danny was off getting new business cards printed somewhere. He said a new card could turn things around. Johnny came into the trailer after the sale. He was happy.

"Hot fuckin' damn! Got another one. We're rollin' now, buddy."

"Great."

"Listen, I'm gonna give Danny his cut when I get back. I

gotta go close a deal right now that's gonna blow everybody's socks off."

"Oh yeah?"

"You know Barney Johnson?"

"Uh, no."

"Of Barney and Joe Johnson Ford?"

"Oh, right."

"They want to front me ten practically new cars and maybe even finance me for my own lot."

"That's great."

"It gets better. They've already given me a cashier's check for ten thousand dollars up front to make a purchase at auction at Round Rock this afternoon. I'm tellin' ya, Barney Johnson loves me. We were both in Korea. He said he's gonna make me some money, an' I told the man he ain't gonna be sorry. Now you just tell Danny—wait. When's Danny gonna be back?"

"I don't know. He just called me on the mobile phone, but I couldn't understand anything he said."

"That's okay. Now, listen. Tell him I'm moving all of these piece-of-shit cars outta here. We got a whole new ball game. I'm gonna have a driver take these down to San Antonio an' we'll sell 'em in Mexico. He should be here any minute. I'm gonna take this ten thousand an' go up to Round Rock an' use it as a down payment. I'll be back tomorrow with some real cars. Some pretty cars. Tell Danny these cars are gonna sell so quick his head'll spin. An' he's gonna get a commission on each one. Okay, I gotta go."

"All right."

"We'll talk at ya."

"Okay."

He got in the Trans-Am and sped away. A large car-carrying truck did show up then and hauled away all the cars. When Danny returned, I repeated what Johnny had told me. I also mentioned he'd sold a car.

"Where's the check? How much did he sell it for?"

"I think three thousand, but he didn't leave a check."

"Why not? Dammit, why didn't you get one?"

"Hey, man, he's your pal."

"Shit. I'm gonna call him."

He punched some buttons on the office phone but just kept putting it on speaker and talking to himself. "Hello? Hello?" Finally he rang Johnny. No answer.

"I'm gonna make him pay me the lease money now. Before he puts the other cars down." He kept punching buttons. "Where is that bastard?"

* * *

The next day the Barney Johnson came into the trailer. He was a tall man in his late sixties with gray hair, a heavy black brow, and a permanent frown. He looked pissed and asked Danny and me if we'd seen Johnny Florida. Danny said no but that he wanted to find him too, because Johnny owed him a lot of money.

"He owes me almost a thousand dollars," Danny said.

"Son," Mr. Johnson said, "he's into me for over ten thousand dollars now. He was supposed to meet my brother, Joe, in Round Rock yesterday, and he never showed up."

Mr. Johnson proceeded to ask Danny suspicious questions as if Danny was in on it with Johnny. Then Mr. Johnson asked me to tell him exactly, word for word, what Johnny had said to me. I told him everything, about how Johnny had come into the trailer bragging about the check, how he was going to buy some good cars, ship the others to San Antonio and Mexico, and that he said he was coming back.

"Oh, he'll come back," Danny said. "He's coming back."

"Don't hold your breath," Mr. Johnson said. Then, just before he walked out the door, he turned and said, "You know, I wondered about that loudmouth son-of-a-bitch. I did." Then he left. Danny sat there with his fake jaw hanging open. He turned to me.

"Don't you have something to do? How come you're always in here? Listen, I've got a wood order for you to take off. I know you can use that hand to prop shit up. Don't tell me you can't. When do you get that cast off?"

"In a couple days."

"Good. That's good."

* * *

Johnny never returned. It was fine with me. It turned cold, though, and that wasn't too great. I started taking off cords of wood, delivering all over town for Danny. Most of the customers ignored me as I carried large, heavy armloads of firewood into their backyards, stacking up a cord. I wore leather gloves and a canvas Carhartt jacket to keep my arms and hands from being cut up. Each delivery could take more than forty-five minutes or longer, depending on how far I had to carry it. Some of the older retired men often watched me working and, bored or lonely, they told me of their lives as I hurriedly but neatly stacked each cord so it wouldn't fall over. One old man told me he was a veteran of World War II, that he had been a German prisoner of war.

"I was a paratrooper," he said. "They dropped us on the wrong side of the Rhine, and we ended up fighting and got captured. I ran out of ammunition and got my throat cut by this German bastard." He pointed to a half-inch-wide, ragged white line of skin that hung down like a necklace below his wrinkled face. "When their captain came, he was pissed that I was still alive. That soldier missed my arteries, so it looked bloody, it looked bad, but I was okay. They ended up having to take me back to a POW camp and stitch me up."

"Really?"

"Yeah, really. Once I got better, I escaped from the POW camp, got back across the Rhine, and found a British unit that rescued me."

"Wow. Jesus." I finished stacking the last piece of firewood. "Okay, sir, that'll be ninety dollars. . . ."

I knew Danny was finally making some money. I usually had about seven or eight deliveries to make, but I could never get them all. Every night after work, I put the day's checks in a zipper bag and locked them in a metal drawer in his desk, right next to his big bag of weed and a loaded .38 pistol. I always came in late at night and was very tired. I would sit there in the fold-out chair before my open trailer door, staring at all the cars driving past on 183, drinking a beer that was as cold as the air around it.

Sometimes I thought of Susan. I even tried to call her one night at Martin's house, but I got her mother, Betty Sue, on the phone instead. She told me that Susan had landed a job on Martin's CBS pilot. She said Susan was only an intern for a week before they started paying her well. She also mentioned how much she liked the new house Susan and I had just started renting together in Travis Heights, which surprised me. She asked me where I was, what I was doing, and, "Now, why are you working out of town again?" I didn't know what Susan had told her. Or if Betty Sue was just pretending, playing dumb, and giving me a chance. She told me she missed me but that Susan *really* missed me. I told her good-bye and hung up. I thought of Susan working on this TV pilot. I pictured her meeting all these new people, laughing, and having fun. Or I thought of her flirting with some emotive handsome smiling guy in her acting class, her hand on his knee, and could feel myself getting pissed. I shut the door, lay down on my cot, and watched the old TV in the corner of the trailer. It got three channels, four counting the UHF if I could tune it in. I was drinking the cheapest beer I could find, a twelve-pack of Buckhorn, and smoking Danny's weed until I passed out.

*　　*　　*

I came in one night and saw that Danny had started to put up a chain-link fence in the shape of a square near the highway. The next day he told me to help him finish with the fence and then string up a bunch of lights in lines running from the top of the fence in zigzags, from side to side, hanging over the space below. When we finished, he hooked up the lights to a Honda generator. A semi came in then, loaded with Christmas trees, and me and the driver and Danny unloaded all of them and stacked them inside the fenced area.

"I'm gonna sell Christmas trees," Danny said. He gave me some address then and sent me out to deliver more wood.

*　　*　　*

I was pushing a wheelbarrow loaded with oak logs into some-one's backyard one night, and I tripped. The wood flew out and hit the cord I'd already stacked and everything fell over. I decided to quit. I reached Danny's Grass and Wood around eight, and I found Danny standing behind a stack of wood taking a piss, a cloud of steam rising from the wet ground.

I walked up to him and took off my gloves. He began com-plimenting me on all the money I was bringing in now.

"Yeah, that's great. Listen, I quit."

He stared at me. "Well, that kind of leaves me high an' dry, don't it?"

"You'll be all right."

"Yeah, but all these wood deliveries. You're bringing in a lot of money. Maybe I could give you a little raise in a couple weeks. Twenty-five cents more an hour or something."

"No, I'm quitting."

"Fifty cents."

"No."

"I can't go any higher."

"Forget it, man."

I started to walk to my trailer, and Danny ran up next to me. "Can't you just give me some notice? Just two more weeks? Just stay till Christmas, man, an' I'll make it worth your while. I promise."

"I don't know. . . ."

"Come on. I'll give you a Christmas bonus. A big one. I took all these orders from people, an' I gotta deliver them now. Come on."

I thought about the bonus. "All right."

He heaped the wood orders on me then for two weeks, trying to cram them all in. Every night my hand was throbbing. I finally told him I was through, and that last day ended up being my longest. I had ten deliveries to make. Danny said he would have liked to help me but he had to stay there and sell Christmas trees. I started at six-thirty that morning and didn't get back to the trailer until ten-thirty that night. I was extremely tired. At the last delivery I quit even stacking the wood. I just threw it in the guy's backyard and left.

I walked into the construction trailer. Danny was sitting down, and I handed him all the checks.

"Oh good," he said. "This is great." He went through the checks while I stood there. The wind blew cold into the trailer. "Is this all of the checks?"

"Yeah, that's all of them."

"I guess you better get on the road then. I moved all of your shit out of the trailer. It's sitting outside."

"Aren't you forgetting something?"

"What?"

"My check."

"I pay you on Fridays. It's Wednesday."

"Yeah, but it's my last day."

Danny rose out of his chair and walked over to the table I was leaning against.

"Well, I tell ya, when somebody quits me an' leaves me inna bind, I usually like to make 'em wait for that check."

"Oh yeah?"

"Yeah. Like I said, I usually make 'em wait. You know, they can go pound sand if they don't like it."

We stared at each other. I could feel my legs starting to shake. I looked away for something nearby to hit him with, but there was only the pumpkin scale, and he'd bolted it to the table. I saw then, out the door, all of the strings of white lightbulbs, moving in the wind, hanging over the Christmas trees. I decided to beg.

"You're really not gonna pay me?"

He shrugged. "Times are tough."

"Yeah, but it's Christmas."

He laughed. "So?"

"So, I thought you were supposed to be a Christian an' all that shit."

He stared at me for a good ten seconds. His pink scars were moving back and forth. "Well, *shit*," he finally said. "Fine, that's just *fine*. I'll give you your check, but you know what, you're lucky. I fired Pete yesterday and didn't pay him at all. You're lucky, man. You don't know how lucky you are." He took out his checkbook. "How much was it? One thirty-five?"

"One fifty-five."

"Are you sure?'

"I'm positive."

"Fine, whatever." He wrote the check and handed it to me. "Here."

"I guess I'm not getting the bonus," I said.

"I guess not."

I looked at the piece of paper. "Is this check good?'

"Hell, yeah, it's good."

I folded up the check, put it in my pocket, and walked out of the trailer. I picked up my bag of clothes off the metal steps, and Danny followed me.

"Listen," he said. "You never stole anything from me. You were a pretty good employee, even though you got a fucked-up hand now. You're still young, though. You're just a kid. Let me know if you wanna deliver St. Augustine for me in the summer. It's pretty easy. You order around a couple of wets, maybe throw a piece of sod every once in a while."

I walked past him and stopped by the silver fence. I stared up again at all the bright white bulbs suspended over the Douglas firs and Scotch pines. "Hey . . ."

Danny walked up beside me. "What?"

"You wouldn't want to give me a Christmas tree, would you?"

"Well, no, not really. . . . I can't give 'em away. Nobody's buying any of them, and they cost me a lot of money."

"Right."

"Besides," he said, "what the hell are you gonna do with a Christmas tree?"

I didn't say anything. I just left. I hadn't even thought about that.

KANSAS

A few miles down from Danny's Grass and Wood the city really started. There was a large strip mall with a Tom Thumb grocery and some other stores. I tried to cash Danny's check inside of the grocery store but the service counter was closed and the cashiers flatly refused. They probably already had several of Danny's hot checks posted on the wall in the manager's office. I ended up sleeping outside on my laundry bag that night, behind the mall in some tall grass above a dry creek. The ground was cold, uncomfortable.

There was a small savings and loan, Texas State Bank, set off as an independent building in that strip mall also. The next morning I briefly thought of robbing it. I didn't have a gun, but you didn't need a gun to rob a bank. All you had to do was pretend you had a gun and clearly insist the teller watch her hands and slowly give you some of the bank's cash and then casually walk out the front door. I thought about it that morning for several minutes. Then I remembered all the ex-cons I had worked with and how only one guy robbing a bank by himself was for dumb-asses who wanted to go to jail for very little money. The whole system was set up to catch you for it. The real money was in running the bank itself from the top down into the ground, which many people were already doing anyway with the savings and loans in 1986. I also remembered that I didn't have a car or even a getaway bicycle.

I couldn't bring myself to call Susan, so I went to a pay phone outside the bank to call my brother, Alton, instead to ask for a ride, and a job. I was lucky to reach him, to find him back home in Texas at his little cabin in Cypress, where he had a phone.

Since he was a freshman in high school, Alton had been working his ass off to make his own money. I mostly worked in grocery store or landscaping jobs to make my money after school, but Alton's work paid more so I started working with him. Alton was friends with Cecil Keith, the oldest son of the well-known and well-liked Keith family in Cypress. The Keiths owned a thousand acres of hardscrabble land they had been working for more than a hundred years, ranching cattle, cutting and selling cedar posts and coastal hay. They lived modestly, but the whole clan worked from dusk to dawn, seven days a week, and they were worth some money. Cecil Keith was a good-natured, strong, and big man who had two silver front teeth and spoke in a high-pitched feminine voice that did not fit with his body. Alton and I worked for him throughout much of high school, hauling hay, cutting cedar posts, selling and delivering firewood. Some days we helped his small crew of laborers from Mexico, who lived on their ranch, to work, feed, and ship the Keith family's cattle.

Alton, though he had nothing close to Cecil's resources, modeled himself somewhat after the young man and started working for himself, finding other rancher's cedar posts, mesquite, or live-oak wood to cut, other people's hay to haul. He was a hard worker, a hustler, which he had learned from both Cecil Keith and our own tough father. Alton started dealing with the Hill Country cedar choppers who lived out in the woods himself, without Cecil Keith, buying their cedar posts and wood for cheap and then reselling it at a profit. Like me, he never wanted to be at home, but, unlike me, he wasn't very good at school or sports. Soon he was staying away from everything and everyone, more and more every year. By the time he barely graduated from high school, Alton had started his own wood-delivery business and moved into a small cabin he rented in the woods that doubled as his office. He had his own cards printed, which he showed me proudly, that simply read "Alton's Wood and Posts" with his phone number underneath.

Alton always seemed to want something more. Either that or maybe he just wanted to escape, to get out of our house, our town, and take off somewhere, anywhere else. While I was reading what I considered literature, Alton was reading every soldier or spy thriller he could find and was heavily drawn to the action-packed 1980s B movies of the Vietnam War. He loved watching the films of Sly Stallone as Rambo or the Chuck Norris movie *Missing in Action* in what little spare time he had. Otherwise he was always working, making more money to buy and trade up for more and bigger trucks, longer trailers, and heavy equipment for much larger jobs.

Just before I went to college, I made even better money with Alton one last summer when he came upon a new business: hauling railroad ties. He had noticed one day, while driving across a railroad crossing in the nearby town of San Marcos, that when the railroad company replaced their old ties, they left hundreds of the old ones scattered for miles down in the grass and ditches along the steel tracks for months at a time. One evening he hooked up a used, thirty-two-foot gooseneck trailer to his wide Chevy dooly pickup, asked me to help him, and he and I loaded up the big trailer by hand for hours, with dozens of good, straight, solid two-hundred-pound-apiece railroad ties. The next week he proceeded to sell all those free ties for fifteen bucks apiece to local nurseries to be used for garden-bed borders, landscaping, and shoring up hills and lawns. They bought every last tie he had, each time we filled up the gooseneck trailer, to the point that he then sought out wholesalers—the people who sold plants, trees, dirt, fertilizers, and other materials to all of the big nurseries in Texas—businesses that wanted even more railroad ties, as many as we could gather, as fast as we could get them.

We got so busy he hired a small crew of three, strong young men from Mexico we found on a corner in San Marcos, and paid them to help us fill the thirty-two-foot gooseneck with heavy ties we stacked and sold to the wholesalers. We were so busy that we forgot that those creosote-covered railroad ties were really the seemingly discarded property of the railroad company, and not ours. One night Alton and I and three other workers were caught gathering ties by two men from the national railroad company that ran and repaired many of the lines, the tracks, through Texas. We were briefly worried, but Alton was a genuine good old boy, and after talking for thirty minutes with the reps from the railroad, their company offered to hire him and his business to pick up all the ties they had discarded and to dispose of them, while allowing him to keep any good ones that he found in the grass to sell or do with what he liked.

Five years later, when I called him from that pay phone, his business was called Texas Cross Ties, and it was pulling in a couple hundred thousand dollars a year through long-term legal contracts with the same railroad company. He was still working seven days a week, but now had three crews of undocumented workers from Mexico and Central America and half a dozen foremen who ran them, two rickety semis to pick up the railroad ties and truck them to nursery and landscaping wholesalers, and a number of big shitty trucks and large tractors, front- end loaders, to pick up the ties and ship orders. His business stretched from far South Texas to Houston, to New Mexico and the high plains, up into Kansas and Nebraska. It was really a miracle I found him at home when I called. His life was now always spent on the road, chasing the next big tie job for the railroad company, and he was about to leave again. He was happy to hear from me though. He came to pick me up in Austin, where we stayed that night at a cheap motel on far South Congress and got drunk on a case of Miller.

*   *   *

The next morning Alton and I drove out of town in an old yellow five-ton flatbed. The truck had holes in the floorboard, and you could see the highway whizzing by under your feet. There was no gas pedal, just a steel rod coming up through the floor. Around two in the morning we stopped in Longview at the Starlight Motel in northeast Texas. The place was a group of run-down bungalows crowded along the highway. We parked the truck, and I followed Alton inside a bungalow.

The walls were cheap, warped paneling. A radio was playing loud *ranchera* music. A short middle-aged man was sitting on a mattress without sheets holding an old suitcase in his lap.

"This is Augustine," Alton said.

Augustine nodded to me and smiled. He had a wide face and a little, thin mustache that ran down around the corners of his mouth. His hair was black and shiny and speckled with white flecks of dandruff. He clutched a knit cap in his hands with the words "Washington Redskins" stitched across it.

"Round everybody up," Alton said. "Let's *vamonos*."

Augustine walked outside and started knocking on bungalow doors. Alton and I trailed behind him. At each bungalow Alton walked inside and yelled, "Everybody get the fuck up! Hurry up! *Vamonos!* Ándale! Let's go!"

Alton had a black beard, long black hair, and a black cowboy hat. He was well over six feet tall and wore cowboy boots. He looked like a giant pirate. The men were sleepy but worried, and they frantically grabbed their clothes.

It was very cold and a long way to Kansas. When everyone was ready, Alton told them to get up on the back of the flatbed. Nine men slowly climbed up and huddled against the cab. Alton and I got inside the truck where the heater was. Before we left, Alton called to Augustine and a seventeen-year-old boy named Juan and told them they could sit inside the truck. Alton explained: "They stink like shit, but Augustine keeps everybody in line. Juan's the best goddamn driver you ever saw. He drives our front-end loaders like a car. I pay him twenty dollars a day. That's more than anybody else out here."

Juan and Augustine squeezed into the cab between us. Their faces were blank, dark, and tired. The men in back jostled one another, talking loudly for a moment. Their voices faded out with sound of the engine, and we left the hotel.

* * *

We drove through flat North Texas. When I was driving, Alton thumbed through his collection of Vietnam War action books, read the novelization of *Rambo: First Blood Part II*, and talked.

"Ya know, Jake, I could survive in the jungle," Alton said.

"Yeah?"

"No, I could do it. I been researchin' it. Readin' up on it."

"Good for you."

I stared at the road. Augustine had fallen asleep and had his heavy head on my shoulder. I looked in the back and saw that the seven other men had stopped moving. Maybe they'd frozen to death. . . .

"See," Alton said, "I've studied it an' I'd know how to survive. How to blend into the jungle and how to kill the gooks. Those guys don't look that tough to me. They're all short as shit. I could pick 'em up an' throw 'em two at a time."

I watched the road.

"You gotta be willing to die, right? I mean, I'm willing to die. I know I can kill 'em. I have to. We need to go back there and get rid of the Russians. The Russians are trying to take over the world."

"Right."

"Tell me this. . . ."

We bounced along the road and drove into Oklahoma. The sun began to rise. There was nothing but dark, flat ground around us.

"Are you listening? Tell me this—"

"What?"

"Okay, what if, say, I went to Thailand on some mercenary kind of thing, an' I was trying to save some POWs an' I, uh . . . I disappeared in the jungle. I was missing. Would you get some people together and come get me?"

"No."

"What if I was tied up in some bamboo cage with rats and no food—"

"A bamboo cage?"

"Right, right, an' I was skinny an' starving an' had been missing for a long time an' everyone knew I was missing. You understand?"

"Yes. You're missing."

"Right, right, I've been gone a long time. Would you get together your friends and come get me?"

"Probably not."

"Come on, I need to know this shit before I go. That I have someone who'll come an' get me."

"Maybe you should take a nap or something."

"I'm gonna bring my AK-47 and my Uzi. They're under the seat. I'll show 'em to you later. They're converted to automatic. I need 'em out here working with these criminals. I carry a lot of cash on me sometimes. Every foreman I got is a scumbag convict. I tell you the white guys and the niggers are the worst. The Mexicans are the only ones you can count on."

"Right."

"All right, I'm gonna take a nap."

He turned over and went to sleep. I got tired of Augustine

leaning on me and nudged him roughly. He grunted once, put his head on Juan's shoulder, and fell back to sleep.

*   *   *

Our base was in Cottonwood Falls, Kansas. Thirty miles south was Cassoday, Kansas. From there we'd work our way back along the railroad tracks. We arrived in Cottonwood Falls in the afternoon and stopped at a motel. It was on the Cottonwood River and called, the Cottonwood Inn. The owner was an old man with big hands and big ears named Mr. Sealy. He showed Alton and me around the motel. He lived in the biggest of the rooms, and we went inside and he introduced us to his wife who was watching some old black and white movie on TV. She sat next to an open gas heater with moving blue flames. Mr. Sealy told us his story.

"I used to be a farmer. I was a farmer all my life. So was my daddy and granddaddy. Everybody was going bankrupt around here, though, so Mary an' I sold the land just in time and bought this motel. We did real good. This is a nice place. There's fishing in the back. They catch big catfish here. Come on."

He led us around the motel down a slope to the wide brown river. There was a tall cottonwood tree on the bank with large rotten catfish heads stuck on hooks embedded in the trunk.

"Look how big these fish were," Mr. Sealy said.

"Those were big fish," Alton said.

Mr. Sealy looked at me and tilted his head, puzzled. He gestured at the trees around the clearing. "Most all of these are pecan trees. Come on in here and look at the garage."

We followed him into a garage that ran lengthwise under several of the rooms. Against the walls there were some farm tools, old tires, and some furniture. The old man walked up to three, round steel tubs full of pecans. He ran his fingers through the brown pecans.

"Look at all these pecans," he said.

"Wow," Alton said.

"Take some. Here." He grabbed many pecans in his big hands and gave them to us.

"Thanks," Alton said.

"Thank you," I said. I broke one open and started eating it.

"I guess we need to check in," Alton said. "I got some cash here. I'll pay you a month in advance for three rooms."

Mr. Sealy smiled and seemed excited. "Okay, fellas, good, okay. Let's go on up to the living room an' I'll get you a receipt."

*　　*　　*

We got up at six every morning. Juan and Augustine were sharing a room with Alton and me. They blared *conjunto* music while cooking a breakfast and lunch of tortillas, eggs, beans, and anything else they could throw in there. Alton and I got up slowly, pulling on stiff, tar-covered clothes, and staggered outside to the truck. The other workers were out there already waiting. No one ever said anything at dawn. They just sat and shivered and dozed. We drove down to Cassoday and started working our way back to Cottonwood Falls, making a mile or so a day.

Alton drove one front-end loader, and Juan drove the other. The rest of us walked along the tracks picking up railroad ties the company had left and stacked them on the forks of the loader. When we had twenty stacked, the driver stopped, raised up the bundle, and Augustine and I ran a steel band around the ties. We tightened the band, put a clip on it, and crimped it. The driver left the bundle in the ditch to be loaded on a flatbed later. The flatbed driver would then take the bundles to a central location in Cassoday or Matfield Green, where the company driver would come by in an 18-wheeler to be overloaded and take the ties away.

From sunup to noon, we stacked the ties on the loaders. Occasionally, a rabbit would dart out from under a pile of ties. Hector and Tomas, the two biggest and quickest men, would catch the rabbits. They'd chase after them, hit them with a rock or a piece of wood, and throw them on the truck to be eaten later. It was very cold out there on the brown plain. None of the men had any coats or jackets. Alton said they were saving their money to buy some warm clothes. Most of their money, he said, went to their families in Mexico. Every one of them, even Juan, had children at home.

At lunch we left them huddled together out on the tracks with their cold tortillas and water and went into Cassoday to have a lunch of steak and potatoes on the company's tab. When we returned, full of beer and food, the men were already back at work, and we joined in. At the end of each week Alton would let another man drive his loader, and ask me to join him for a walk down the tracks to find elusive ties hidden in the tall grass. We'd walk for miles, hours, down the endless tracks. Yellow-and-brown fields flanked us, and a wide blue sky covered our heads. We said nothing. We walked quietly, searching the grass, or we stared at the converging rails and tripped over rocks.

When it was too dark to see, every night, Alton would shut off his tractor's engine, and all the men would drop their loads and gather around the flatbed. It seemed very quiet then, without the engines and shouts and orders. We loaded into the truck, silent and tired, and drove back to Cottonwood Falls. The men butchered their rabbits and ate. Alton and I drove in to a restaurant in Strong City where there was a liquor store. We ate, then went to the liquor store, and stocked up on beer and whiskey. Back at the motel I would soak in the tub and drink from the bottle and try to wash the creosote off my hands and arms. Alton and I were so tired and sore, we just sat in the room, got drunk, and watched TV. By ten-thirty Alton passed out on the bed. I passed out on the fold-out couch. Before I knew it, Augustine's radio was blaring, his breakfast frying, and he was dressed and loudly telling Alton to get up.

After a month the 18-wheeler came into Cassoday one evening, and Alton got on his machine. The driver told me his name was George. He was short and pudgy and balding, with blond eyelashes. He smiled when he talked and had a tic in his right eye. He and I sat in the cab and talked while Alton loaded the ties. We drank a few beers and smoked a joint. He told me he was a Vietnam vet, a portrait artist, and an alcoholic.

"I know I'm an alcoholic," he said. "I've been to AA. That's the first step, admitting you're one. I just can't get past that, though. I did two tours, volunteered for the second one, and got shot in the stomach by someone I never saw. As soon as I got back to San Francisco, I got arrested for riding inside of a drier in a laundromat two nights in a row. My wife an' I live in Texas now. We got a trailer out in Giddings, but I'm building my own house. I keep getting DUIs, but Alton's been good to me. I need this job."

That night George and Alton and I took the flatbed into Strong City and went to the liquor store. I bought a bottle of whiskey and we drove back to Cottonwood Falls. No one was on the small cobblestone streets. We saw bright lights on the edge of town and drove toward them. It was a high-school football game, and hundreds of people and cars from miles around surrounded the isolated stadium. We parked the truck and sat on a cold bench outside the bleachers and watched the lights and crowd and listened to the noise. We passed around the whiskey, and Alton began to ask George questions about Vietnam and the things he'd seen there, and George gave him some answers.

Alton grew quiet as he told him of the realities of the Vietnam War, which were a little different from his Chuck Norris movies. "I was afraid, man," George said. "Everybody was scared shitless all the fucking time. You never knew what was gonna kill you, or who, or where the VC even was. Some jackass who came in and did the laundry in the morning at the base would shoot you in the head that night or blow your balls off with a booby trap in the jungle in the afternoon. I mean, shit, I used to fill up my pack with as many grenades as I could carry before we went out on patrol. And I just threw them at everything in sight, any sound I heard. I didn't give a fuck what it was. I wanted the napalm to burn that whole country down so I could at least see who was trying to kill me. Either that or you were bored out of your mind, sitting there with crotch rot eating cans of C rations, waiting for another round of bullshit. . . ."

I got off the bench and let them talk, lying down on the cold concrete, drinking the whiskey. I stared up at the black sky and yawned, watching my breath move away and disappear.

*   *   *

The next day there was a storm at work. A huge cold front was barreling in and the rain was beating down on us and we were slipping and falling in the mud and the ditches were filling with water, but Alton insisted we keep on working. I finally went up to him on his loader and told him we should go in.

"Let's just get a few more ties," he said. "Come on—"

Just then lightning struck a lone tree right next to us and the flatbed and the metal rails. There was an incredibly loud noise, and I saw the white bolt hit the tree and move in a spiral down its trunk, leaving it smoking and charred. Alton jumped so much he almost fell out of the tractor down onto me. "I guess we better go in," he said.

Juan, Augustine, Alton, and I climbed inside the truck. The seven other men hopped on the flatbed and crowded against the cab, but there was no escape from the rain. They were all soaking wet and freezing, but they were laughing and shouting and smiling. It was our first day off in weeks. Before we started the truck, lightning struck again extremely close, and everyone jumped. Augustine began to yell at Alton in Spanish.

"All right, I'm goin', I'm goin'!" Alton said. He started the truck, shifted gears noisily, and we drove back to the motel.

*   *   *

I called Susan that night at a pay phone down the street, standing out there in the rain. I wanted to hear her voice. She sounded happy and said she hadn't been doing much.

"Pat's here."

"Yeah? What's she doing?"

"She's taking a nap right now. She came in to get an abortion this afternoon."

"God, what is that, four?"

"Five."

"Can't she get a diaphragm or something?'

"I guess she's very fertile."

"I guess."

"We're going to a party later."

I hesitated briefly. "Tonight?"

"Yeah."

"Whose party?"

"Well, you remember Dwayne?"

"Of course."

"I ran into him the other day—"

"Ran into him?"

"At the Kash n' Karry in Clarksville. Anyway, he's got these two guys, the Jacobs brothers, who were students in his film class, and they've actually got some money and a script together with my uncle Martin—"

"Martin's involved with this?"

"He cowrote the screenplay and has a producer credit."

"I heard 'we' moved to Travis Heights."

"It's a cute, cheap little house, Jake, just off Alta Vista. I really think you'd like it, babe, if you'd just come home."

"So Dwayne's making a real movie?"

"Oh no, not at all. It's his old film students from UT, these young guys, the Jacobs brothers. Terry Jacobs is the writer, and Aaron Jacobs is the director. They made this small independent film in Austin last year, and it got their foot in the door. They have this script, this highbrow Western they wanna do, and Martin's helping them turn it into a miniseries."

"TV?"

"Yeah, but good TV, big TV. ABC bought it."

"ABC."

"It's real money, Jake."

"I bet it is."

"Look, Martin asked me if I wanted to work on it, and I said yeah."

"He get you a part in it?"

"Well, no, not acting."

"What happened to that?"

"I don't know. Maybe that wasn't such a good idea. Dwayne's got a little part in it as an extra, can you believe that?"

"Playing what?"

"A drunk cowboy in a whorehouse. He even has a line."

"He's on his way. So what're you gonna do?"

"Martin said he could get me a job in the production department, as a production secretary or maybe as an assistant to the UPM—"

"The what?"

"The unit production manager, the UPM, who's also doubling as the line producer on this miniseries."

"Listen to you."

"Yes, listen to me. I'm doing this. And you can come with

me." She paused. "I talked to Martin about getting you a job on it, too."

"Susan, you didn't have to do that."

"I wanted to. Seriously, I talked to him and he introduced me to the production designer who introduced me to the head scenic for the whole series—"

"What's that?"

"He's basically the painter of all the sets, or he's in charge of all of the set painters and artists who do all of the faux finishes, fake backgrounds and stuff. They're gonna build an entire old Western town out in New Mexico, near Sante Fe. He told me they have a big budget—"

"The head scenic?"

"Yeah, and get this—"

"What?"

"He says he needs a set painter, but it needs to be, this is a direct quote, 'a *smart* person who can both paint *and* draw.' I mean, come on, Jake, how perfect could that be for you?"

"I don't know."

"Your pay would be nine hundred dollars a week."

"You're shitting me. Nine hundred a week?"

"Right, *and* you'll get per diem, room and board. It's *twice* what I'm making in the production office."

"For how long?"

"For the whole movie, the whole miniseries, like four months."

"Damn. Nine hundred a week—"

"Should I tell him yes?"

"Let me think about it."

"You better think quick. Preproduction starts in just a few weeks. The whole crew is going to Sante Fe."

"Are you going too?"

"I'll be in Austin working for the production coordinator, who's working for this British line producer, Ian Watt, so you'll have to go first. But I'll be right behind you. I'll come in right before shooting starts, and we can be together again. Okay?"

"Yeah, maybe. . . . "

We were silent for a while. I could hear the wet sound of a car passing on the street behind me.

"Well?"

"Well. . . . Have fun at your party."

"Are you mad?"

"No."

Silence again.

"Why are you doing this?"

"I don't know."

"I miss you."

"Yeah, I miss you, too. I guess I'll see you later."

"Okay."

I hung up the phone, stood there for a second, and then walked down the empty street back to the motel. I walked into my room and found Alton watching TV and reading a Conan comic book. He looked up, a smile on his face.

"What's wrong?"

"Nothing." I grabbed a beer out of an ice chest on the floor and opened it and sat at the table.

"What's the matter?"

"Don't worry about it, Alton. Just watch your stupid show."

His smile disappeared. "This ain't a stupid show, all right? It's *Magnum, P.I.*, the best detective show on TV."

"Sorry, my mistake."

*   *   *

Because of all the rain the night before, Alton announced that we wouldn't have to work the next day. The ground was too muddy for the machines. We slept and drank and watched TV all day and then walked down to the one bar in town after dinner. They had several pool tables and some 3.2 beer. All of the men had followed us and Alton offered to buy the workers as much beer as they wanted and everyone seemed happy. The owner of the bar was a tall, white-haired man in a cowboy hat. Alton said he didn't like him: "He's too nice to the wetbacks. He's giving them a big head."

We played pool and drank. Augustine challenged Alton to a game of pool and beat him easily. The owner, the old cowboy, was getting drunk, and he invited us into the back room and we followed, swaying and bloated from 3.2 beer. It was a large white room with a high ceiling. In the middle of the floor there was a mechanical bull. Along one wall were several fold-out chairs. A one-armed man with a beard and cap sat in a chair holding a control box. The cowboy yelled to him, "Virgil! These boys wanna ride the bull."

Virgil looked excited. "They do?"

"Hell, yeah."

The cowboy put his arm around a drunk Augustine. "Come on, son, you can do it."

Augustine smiled and shook his head forcefully and said no, and everyone laughed.

The cowboy tried to persuade Juan and the others to ride, but they all shook their heads and laughed and said no. "Aw come on, boys," he said. "Even Virgil can ride it."

Hector and Tomas, the two strongest workers, came into the room then, and Hector, without hesitation, walked over to the mechanical bull and hopped up on it.

"Ahh, we got a *vaquero* here," the cowboy said. "Let 'er rip, Virgil, and keep it on low."

Virgil started the machine up, and Hector was thrown around but stayed on. Everyone cheered, and Hector stepped off triumphantly.

"I gotta do this now, I guess," Alton said and he climbed up on the fake bull, his long legs almost touching the ground. Virgil started up the machine at the same speed, and Alton immediately fell off. Virgil stopped the bull, Alton got back on, and this time he made it. When it stopped he said, "Move it up a notch."

"Here we go," Virgil said. "Hang on."

He managed to stay on but was very pale when the machine stopped. "I'm gettin' dizzy," he said. "Turn it up another notch."

"You got it," Virgil said.

Alton came close to falling off and he twisted his arm but he stayed on. When it was over he got off the machine in pain. "I think I broke my hand," he said.

Hector walked up, hopped on the mechanical bull, yelled "Go!" and rode with ease, as though he'd ridden real bulls for years. When eight seconds were up, he motioned for Virgil to turn up the machine all the way and gave Alton a challenging look.

The old cowboy and Augustine were holding each other up and cheering Hector on. "*Cuidado*, Hectorito!" the cowboy yelled.

The room grew quiet then, and Hector braced himself, raised one arm in the air, and gave a somber nod. He almost made it, but one of the last turns threw him straight off the bull and into the wall. He scraped his cheek badly, leaving a streak of blood on the white plaster. The cowboy closed it down. "Let's go play pool," he said. "You boys're gonna get hurt in here."

We followed him back into the poolroom. An ugly obese young girl was now sitting at the bar, and Hector and Tomas started talking to her. The other men went to the tables, and Alton and I stumbled back to our room at the motel. We were woken up around three in the morning.

"What's that noise?" Alton asked. "I hear yellin' goin' on."

Somebody started banging on the door. Alton got out of bed and opened it. It was the owner, Mr. Sealy. He had his cap in his hands. I stood up, and the room was spinning. I walked to the front door and tried not to throw up.

"I didn't want to call the sheriff," he said. "I really didn't. But they wouldn't keep quiet."

Alton was still trying to wake up. "What?"

"I couldn't get ahold of you. You wouldn't answer the door."

Augustine and Juan slowly got out of bed then and mechanically pulled on their clothes. Juan started to fix breakfast. I looked out the door and saw the sheriff's car. Blue-and-red lights moved back and forth across Mr. Sealy's face.

"What happened?" Alton asked.

"I heard screaming, and I didn't know what was going on. I

tried to get the door open, but they got it braced or something. They're making too much noise. I'm sorry, but that's just too much. I had to call the sheriff. One of them threw a bottle out the back window. You're gonna have to pay for that window."

We went outside, and the sheriff got out of his car. He walked up to the room next to ours and said to Alton, "These're your men, right?"

"Yessir," Alton said. "I don't know what the problem is, sheriff."

"They're drunk and tearing the place up. That's the problem. Now they won't open the door."

"They're gonna pay for the damages," Mr. Sealy said.

Alton reassured him. "It's okay, we will, Mr. Sealy."

"We need to get that door open," the sheriff said.

Mr. Sealy wrung his cap. "My wife and I heard a girl screaming."

"All right," Alton said. He knocked on the door lightly. "Tomas? Hector?" There was the sound of furniture being moved, scraped across the floor. Alton looked at me and yelled out, "Tomas! Hector! Cristóbal! Open the goddamn door!"

No answer. Augustine walked up then and indicated to Alton that he would take care of it. Normally reserved, Augustine was still drunk, and he began to kick the door and bang on it while screaming in Spanish at the men inside, and someone, Cristóbal, quickly opened it. Augustine shoved him out of the way roughly, and Cristóbal tripped backward and hit the floor. Alton, the sheriff, Mr. Sealy, and I crowded one after the other into the front room. Mr. Sealy dropped his cap.

"Oh my God," he said. His big ears turned red. "Oh my God!"

Blood was spattered all over the walls in the little kitchen area.

"What did they do?" Mr. Sealy asked. His eyes were open wide. The sheriff pulled out his gun. Alton and I walked to the sink and saw a couple of bloody rabbit skins.

"It's just rabbit blood, Mr. Sealy," Alton said. "They've been skinnin' rabbits here."

Mr. Sealy picked up his cap, and the sheriff knocked loudly on the closed door that led to the back room.

"Dammit, you're gonna pay for this!" Mr. Sealy yelled at Alton. "There's blood all over this place. These walls are ruined. I want a new paint job, and you're gonna pay for it."

"Okay," Alton said calmly. "Don't worry, Mr. Sealy, I promise I'll pay for everything."

A few men had been passed out on the front beds when we barged in. They were sitting up now, still and frozen, staring at the sheriff's gun. We heard voices behind the door, someone laughing, and Augustine grew angry again and kicked the door and yelled in Spanish. One of the men, Miguel, slowly opened the door, and the sheriff pushed through and we followed him in, filling the small room with people. Miguel was in his underwear and tried to run out past us. Augustine grabbed him and suddenly started beating him, hitting him on the back and in the face. The sheriff put up his gun, and he and I pulled Augustine off Miguel. Alton started yelling at Augustine and said, "Take it easy, goddammit! Leave him alone, Augustine!"

Then I saw the young woman from the bar lying naked on the bed. She was drunk and flabby and pale white. Only her head was small and had some color. It looked like a little pumpkin. She was giggling. Hector and Tomas were both naked, next to her. They were quiet and staring at us. They didn't appear to be particularly worried, just surprised.

Alton turned to Mr. Sealy and said angrily, "Shit, this is why you called the sheriff?"

"They were making too much noise. There was screaming. I didn't know what was happening."

The sheriff was pissed and yanked the fat girl out of the bed. "Get your goddamn clothes on, Katy! Let's go! Come on, girl."

The young woman was drunk and laughing. The sheriff helped her get dressed and took her out to the car. Augustine began to berate Hector and Tomas, who had covered themselves with the sheets and were staring at the floor.

"Okay, that's enough," Alton said and he led Augustine out of there back to our room. "Go back to sleep, Augustine."

The sheriff walked up and asked Mr. Sealy if everything was settled now.

"They gotta pay for these damages," Mr. Sealy said.

"Okay, okay, we will," Alton said.

"And I want you to check out by Monday," Mr. Sealy said. "I got some nice people coming up, and I can't have all this trouble going on."

"Fine," Alton said.

I went back to my fold-out couch then and fell asleep to the sounds of Alton yelling at the men next door.

* * *

I was standing at the top of an embankment on the edge of the railroad tracks. It was a cold, clear day, and the wind was blowing hard from the north. I watched large groups of black and brown cowbirds flying down into the yellow fields in the distance. They seemed to stretch for miles, and as soon as one group of birds had hit the ground, another would explode upward, into the air, each bird swerving and dipping at the same time, like a giant swarm of bees changing shapes in the sky.

I watched the men working down in the ditch. All of them were hard at it except the one, Hector. He dragged along, doing very little except talk, slowing down his partner, Tomas, with each tie. He noticed me watching him and tipped his cap back and said something in Spanish I couldn't understand. Alton was driving the big machine, and the engine droned loudly. The men slowly bent to the ground again and again, hauling out the good ties from the dead grass, stacking them on the forks of the loader, and banding them in steel. Next pile. Tomas struggled with a tie embedded in the dirt while Hector sat down on the edge of the hill and spoke to him as he worked. I walked down the embankment and grabbed the tie Tomas had been struggling with, picked it up myself, and threw it sloppily onto the forks. I looked over to Hector and yelled, "Come on, let's go! Get off your ass!" Alton shouted down from the loader above, "Move your fucking ass, Hector! Quit fucking around!" I yelled to Hector to pick up the end of a heavy tie. He hesitated. "Pick it up, goddammit!" I yelled, and picked up my end. He lifted the other, and we threw it on the forks. I quickly grabbed another one, and Hector got the other end and we tossed it on. Before I could get to the next tie, he was there. We tossed it on, and I ran to the next pile and Hector ran behind me. Soon we were ahead of all the other workers and still kept going, just him and me and Alton and the loader. We worked for six hours, steadily, until it was almost dark, and then we stopped. I struggled up the embankment to the rails. I saw a long line of brown bundles scattered through the ditches. The sky was turning from blue to black with only a thin line of red left on the horizon. Alton pulled up and cut the engine on his loader. Juan stopped the engine on his machine, and there was only a steady humming then and the wind. Everyone lined up in front of the water cooler on the flatbed except Hector, who walked off into the distance and sat down on a bundle of ties, alone.

"That's the way I like to see 'em work," Alton said. "We threw more ties today than any other day. That's how you do it."

I filled a dirty paper cup with water and took a drink.

*　*　*

The next morning, Alton and I drove to Cassoday to get some repairs done on the flatbed. We left the men working at the tracks with Augustine in charge. On the way down I told Alton I was quitting, and he looked surprised.

"But why? You're just getting into it."

"No, I'm not."

"Okay, fine," he said, and I could see he was angry. "I knew you wouldn't last more than a month. I knew you'd quit. You're going back to her."

"Right. When's your next run to Texas?"

"Four months. I have to go to Oklahoma after this in about three weeks."

We rode along for a while in silence.

"I guess I need to find a ride," I said.

Alton stared at the road. "I guess so," he said.

We rode quietly the rest of the way to Cassoday. When we pulled into the little town, Alton stopped at the mechanic's shop and I walked down to the Cassoday Café, a small, clapboard building with a warped and tilting front porch. I opened the door, and a bell rang lightly. I sat at the counter on a round stool. The waitress appeared from the back, and I ordered a cup of coffee and some toast. She brought me the toast and poured some coffee.

"You want some jelly?" she asked.

"No thanks."

"Strawberry preserves?"

"Okay."

She brought me two packets of preserves, and I opened one and spread it on the toast. She left, and I ate and drank. The café was empty. I could hear the waitress and cook talking in low voices in the kitchen. I stared at the cups and white dishes stacked on shelves in front of me. I looked at the glass pie container filled with slices of fruit pie. The waitress came back out and smiled and raised her eyebrows. "You want some more coffee?"

"No thanks, I gotta go."

"That'll be two bucks."

I pulled three crumpled dollars out of my pocket and laid them on the counter. "Thanks."

"Okay, thank you," she said and picked up my plate and cup.

I got up off the stool and walked out the front door. I stopped at the edge of the wood porch. The sky was covered in low gray clouds. I looked to my left and saw the gas station and mechanic's shop and a white church across the road. To my right there were a couple of empty shops, and the main street turned to dirt and ended. Directly in front of me, off an asphalt road full of holes, there sat a blue trailer. It was an old Airstream with rounded edges and odd fifties windows. A large leaning antenna stood up on the roof. All around the trailer's base someone had nailed latticework and painted it gray. The door of the trailer opened, and a small boy ran out. He was nine or ten, lanky, with red hair, a T-shirt, and jeans. He ran around the lawn chasing a little cat and then hopped on a bike. He rode in circles on the asphalt road and headed in my direction. As he rode past the porch of the Cassoday Café he gave me a big wave.

"Hi!" he yelled.

I waved back and watched him ride up the street, past the white church, and up the road until he disappeared. I looked over the church's steeple and on a hill saw a large brown sign. It read:

You are in Cassoday, Kansas.
The Prairie Chicken Capital of the World!

I walked down the porch steps and went over to the mechanic's shop. Alton was in there playing a pinball machine.

"Is the truck ready?" I asked.

"Almost."

I bought a few pieces of beef jerky from the mechanic's wife. I ate them and read about all the bankruptcy sales and farm auctions posted on the walls. The mechanic came out of the garage and said the truck was ready. Alton paid the man, we climbed in the truck and drove back toward Cottonwood Falls.

*   *   *

A few days later a company foreman from Nebraska came through town on his way to set up the job in Oklahoma. The guy's name was Ed, and he said he'd give me a ride as far as Tulsa. It was late afternoon when he stopped by the motel, and Alton was out loading up a truck in town.

Ed and I drove down to Matfield Green, and I found Alton in a field full of tie bundles, on his tractor, loading up George's 18-wheeler. George and I talked for just a second, and I told Alton we were leaving right then. He said nothing and ignored me. I asked him if he could mail me my last check and handed him a piece of paper with a PO box in Texas, and he took the paper and again said nothing. George said good-bye to me, said he was going north now, but that I should stop by some-time in Texas, and he gave me his address in Giddings.

"I'll paint your portrait," he said.

As I got in the truck with Ed, Alton suddenly cut the engine, jumped off the loader, and ran over to the truck. I rolled down my window. Alton took off his gloves, reached in, and shook my hand.

"Thanks for working with me up here."

"Sure."

"It gets kinda lonely sometimes."

"Thanks for the job. I needed the money."

He stood there, uncomfortable, at the edge of the truck, look-ing away. "Listen, uh . . . you ever see anybody down there?"

"No, not really."

He looked down at the ground and kicked a rock. "Well, if you do, tell 'em I said hello, okay?"

"Okay."

He looked up at me, from under his black wide-brimmed hat, and I could see my own features in his face.

"Look, don't worry," I said. "I'll come get you."

He smiled then, happy again, and walked off, putting on his gloves.

I rolled up the window, and Ed started to turn the big truck around. I looked back and saw Alton standing next to the loader in the empty field, watching us leave.

"Let's go up to the liquor store in Strong City," Ed said. "We can get some real beer there. All they have is that near-beer crap for miles."

"All right."

We bought a case of beer in town and then started south for Oklahoma across the flat black land. We drove, stopping every once in a while to take a piss, and Ed talked quite a bit, about his time in prison, how he'd dropped ceilings before he ran into Alton in a bar in Nebraska and landed the foreman job, how he had a girlfriend in Iowa and that he was bringing her down to stay with him in Tulsa. That he thought she was pregnant. I could see a scattered line of lights from some distant town on the horizon, disappearing and reappearing as we topped each rise, and Ed talked and talked, but I figured that was okay. It was his life, and I couldn't really blame him for being interested in it.

SWEETHEART OF THE RODEO

I was lying on my bed, staring at a water stain on the ceiling, when my mother-in-law called and invited me to join her and her new friend, Karen, at the annual Fourth of July rodeo in Cypress. She asked if I'd had dinner, and I said yes. She said so had they and, if I'd like, I should drive out right then as the rodeo was starting in two hours. I heard laughter in the background and asked what they were doing. My mother-in-law mentioned once again how it was imperative that I leave now, that they had a box, that BH and Denny Hit were coming, that Denny Hit was a former bull-riding champion from Victoria, and that she was wearing the gray boots rather than the brown. I promised to be there and hung up.

I went into the bathroom and, using pliers, turned on the cold water. I shaved and then stood in front of the mirror for a few minutes and practiced smiles and greetings.

"Hi," I said, smiling broadly.

"Hi, how's it going?"

"It's nice to meet you."

I quickly left the bathroom and changed into a pair of jeans, boots, and a freshly starched purple shirt. I went to the kitchen and filled a blue bowl on the floor with dry cat food. I watched our cat, Jack, attack the mound of food.

"What do you think of this shirt, Jack?"

The cat opened his mouth wide and shook his head with each bite, flinging little brown squares onto the linoleum.

"I think it's too purple."

I went out onto the front porch. The sun was setting in front of our little house in Travis Heights. A man across the street was fertilizing his lawn. A boy and girl in bathing suits ran shrieking from a sprinkler's arc. In the evening light the shirt appeared more blue than purple, and I decided to go with it. I let the cat out, locked the house, and left for Cypress.

*   *   *

I noticed a few more antique shops on the town square. A new, larger Baptist church. The VFW Hall had expanded its facilities with a high pole barn and concrete pavilion for dances. There was a new white limestone high school, two new limestone strip centers, a new limestone Dairy Queen, and a new limestone bowling alley just across the road from my mother-in-law's house.

I turned into the deeply rutted caliche drive, past the faded No Trespassing signs, and parked in the driveway under the balcony. I walked up the steep limestone steps to the front door. At the top I checked my reflection in the dining-room windows. Passing muster, I used the knocker. There was no answer, and I let myself in the house.

I called out "Betty Sue!" twice and heard nothing. I walked past a painting of blue-and-red apples and into the den. Through the floor-to-ceiling windows, uneven green hills could be seen stretching out to the horizon. Between the hills and the balcony deck there was an orange Sunshine Dry Cleaners sign and a gigantic red-and-white neon bowling pin.

I turned around and saw, like a person standing against the wall, a large portrait of Dean Hampton in a green jacket and yellow cowboy hat, his thumbs hooked defiantly in his pockets. A shotgun leaned in the corner next to the painting. I walked to the bookshelves and read all the titles. I found an old pair of multifaceted rose-colored glasses, put them on, and thumbed through a book called *The Impressionists* lying on the coffee table. I took the glasses off and put them back exactly where I'd found them. There were decorations around the fireplace: melted candles, a clay church from Mexico, Guatemalan worry dolls, and a picture of the Bhagwan pointing serenely to the sky. A Norfolk pine and several pencil cacti were growing wildly from their small pots, tipping them over to the point of danger.

I bent to a bottom shelf, pulled out a photo album, and looked at some pictures: Dean in a black tuxedo seated in a chair, his long hair brushed back from his high forehead, his eyes at half mast, a handsome closed mouth and crooked smile, with Betty Sue standing regally beside him in a long black evening gown, her hand on his shoulder, her long dark hair pulled back into a bun, her face placid, calm, unreadable. An awkward picture of Susan and me at the 1979 junior prom, before a silver curtain. I was wearing a garish white tuxedo, my hair a curly long brown mass, my arm around Susan next to me. She was smiling wildly, wearing too much makeup, a corsage, and a low-cut puce satin dress with spaghetti straps

barely hanging from her thin shoulders. I put the album back
and went through two others. After a few minutes I put the
albums back on the shelf and left the den. I walked through
the dining room, my boots echoing on the pink Saltillo tile,
through the living room, past the open louver doors, into the
master bedroom.

A short, thin, pretty woman walked toward me, examining
her nails. She jumped, her hand to her mouth. "Oh!"

"Sorry."

Betty Sue touched my arm, turned her head, and I gave her
a kiss on the cheek.

"You scared me to death. We're trying on clothes. Karen,
come here."

A voice from the bathroom: "Just a minute, please."

Betty Sue posed in front of me. She raised her hands, palms
up, and smiled. "Well?"

"You look great."

She wore gray boots, a jean skirt, a jean shirt, a silver
iguana or some type of lizard pin, and a bolo tie. I silently
appreciated the outfit but stayed too long on the bolo and
new curly hair.

"The bolo's too much, isn't it? I just got a perm today. It
will take three days to look as it should. So until Monday I'm
in perm limbo. You look very nice, dear. Very tan and healthy
and handsome."

"Thanks."

"Are you healthy? Is your stomach okay?"

She turned to enter the bathroom as I answered.

"Oh yeah, I'm doing great—"

From the bathroom: "Go on, I'm listening," then, to the

invisible Karen, "Put this on, no wait, this," and back to me, "You're doing great?"

I sat down in a leather chair facing away from the windows and toward the bathroom. An altar of assorted Mexican bric-a-brac rose from the chest of drawers beside me.

"I'm doing absolutely great."

"Good. We're all great, *and*"—she added brightly—"we're all cute."

"Great."

"What do you think of these earrings?'

Betty Sue stepped out, slightly different from purple eye shadow and two simple diamonds hanging heavily from her earlobes.

"I think they're great."

"Great. Well, *I* think it's time to go, but *Karen*, my new *best* friend, is taking for*ever*."

"Okay, okay, I'm ready," Karen said, and came into the bedroom.

"Karen, this is my son-in-law, Jake Stewart."

"Hi."

"Hi, Jake Stewart," Karen said, dragging out the *s* sound. She smiled and pulled her hair back into a ponytail.

I stared at her face, my mouth open slightly. Betty Sue sighed loudly and walked from the room saying we were late and that she could absolutely not find her purse. Karen promised just a second and turned to retrieve one last article from the bathroom. I saw, then, that in the flurry of rodeo preparation she'd forgotten to zip up the back of her blue jean skirt. I also couldn't help noticing she'd neglected to put on any underwear. I sat back down in the leather chair and watched her bend over to fill a small purse and adjust the loose-fitting vest she wore without a shirt. After a few seconds she said, "Okay" quietly, turned, smiled at me again, and left the room.

Halfway to the kitchen, walking behind her, I cleared my throat.

"Karen, I don't think you're quite finished yet."

She stopped. "What?"

"Your skirt."

She touched the bare skin through her open zipper. "Oh my God," she said. "I'm so embarrassed." She backed into the kitchen.

I waited a moment in the living room. I heard Betty Sue gasp, pause, and then ask if I'd be a dear and carry the garbage down to the garage for her. I said of course, and that one of the constants in my life was taking the garbage out of her house.

I carried the two green bags from the kitchen out of the house. Betty Sue locked the front door. I followed her and Karen, their skirts zipped, down the steps and past the front yard. Weeds had taken over the St. Augustine. A bad freeze had killed the yuccas lining the drive. The plants hung limp, brown, and dead over the limestone retaining wall. I shoved the garbage bags into full cans in the garage and squeezed into the back seat of Betty Sue's Toyota.

"This is going to be so much fun," Betty Sue said.

"It is. I can't wait," Karen said.

They both turned and looked at me expectantly.

"Oh yeah," I said, and tried to sound enthused. "It'll be great."

There was a long silence as we bounced along the driveway. I broke it by mentioning to Betty Sue that the last time I'd seen her she'd been wearing the same jean shirt. She said she knew, and that she'd become too dependent on the shirt, but hadn't I been wearing the same shirt I wore tonight in Santa Fe, too? I said yes, she was right, but that I cared for my shirt in a way she didn't.

"Didn't Susan buy you that?"

"Yeah, she did."

"Now, where is Susan again?" Karen asked.

"She's out of town," I said. "Out of the country, actually."

"She's visiting a friend of ours in San Miguel," Betty Sue said. "Tina Lambert. She used to be married to Bill Lambert, the artist."

"Oh," Karen said.

"Tina teaches art, mainly watercolor painting down there. Susan's taking a class for two weeks."

"Oh," Karen said again. "That sounds like fun."

"She just got off work," I said, then added, "She needed a vacation."

"Jake and Susan just finished working on the TV Western miniseries *The Cry of the Plain*. It's coming out in '88, and it's going to be incredibly popular. Jake, do you have a roach?"

I checked my pockets and said no.

"Maybe I can find one in the ashtray," Betty Sue said.

Karen turned in her seat and faced me. "What did you do on it?"

"I was one of the painters. We painted the sets."

"Oh, neat," Karen said.

"Susan was an assistant to the producer, Ian Watt," Betty Sue said. "He's from England, but he lives in Dallas. Ian has a fabulous art collection. He's a new friend of Martin's."

"I think I've heard of Ian Watt," Karen said. "I think Martin gave Ian one of my pies."

"Karen makes the *best* pies," Betty Sue said and looked into the rearview mirror to delicately remove something from her eye.

"Is there anything wrong?" Karen asked.

"No," Betty Sue said, "I've just got some dust in my contact." She went back to rummaging through the ashtray, driving the car, and blinking her left eye over and over until a tear formed. "Ahh, here's one. Jake, dear, would you please light it?"

"Sure."

I took the large roach from her hand, and Betty Sue's fingers lingered noticeably on my own, her gaze meeting mine. She smiled, pulled away, and handed me a roach clip.

"And here."

I lit it and we passed it back and forth, filling the car with smoke. Karen politely refused the first two passes. Betty Sue mentioned how Karen was incredibly healthy and didn't smoke or drink or eat sugar, salt, or fat.

"She does all of Martin's cooking since the bypass."

I nodded. "Really."

"I just cook the same food for him that I eat," Karen said.

Betty Sue let out a cloud of gray smoke. "Can't you just tell she's healthy? She's beautiful. Look at her skin, it glows."

"It does," I said and began to cough. Betty Sue started hacking as well, and we formed a chorus. On the third pass, Karen said she would take a hit.

Betty Sue laughed. "I'm shocked."

Karen smiled. "Well, I don't want to be a drag. Besides, I *am* from California." She pursed her lips and inhaled lightly.

She tried to hand the roach to me, and I signaled no more. Betty Sue took it, had one last big hit, and put it out in the ashtray. I stared at the fine blonde hairs on Karen's cheek, then at Betty Sue's blue eyes in the rearview mirror. I saw her full lips part, her mouth open.

"Martin's written the first draft of a new screenplay. I mean a *very* rough draft, and he just dumped the whole thing in my lap yesterday and told me to fix it up." Her words seemed too loud and hung in the fog of the car.

"You poor thing," Karen said.

Betty Sue pouted out her bottom lip. "Poor me. . . . BH and Denny Hit are going to get there at seven-thirty or eight. It's BH's box."

We turned off the ranch road and wound quietly through Briarcreek, a resort development that appeared to be deserted.

"I'm surprised they have boxes now," I said.

"It's changed," Betty Sue said.

"Do they still have slack time?"

"I don't know. We'll have to see." She stared out the windshield. We left Briarcreek, crossed a bridge, and turned at a sign that read: VFW Local 337, Parking.

"What's slack time?" Karen asked.

"It's really the best part of the rodeo," I said. "At the end, all the bull riders who didn't—"

"We're here," Betty Sue said. "This is going to be fun." She parked the car and asked Karen how she looked.

"You look wonderful," Karen said. "How do I look?"

"Very pretty," Betty Sue said drily and began to go through her purse. "You know I haven't been to the rodeo here in so long."

"I thought you said you and BH went last year," Karen said.

Betty Sue laughed. "Oh, I guess we did. Well, it *seems* like it's been forever. I'm going to leave my purse in the car."

"I'm taking mine," Karen said. "It's so small."

"And it's mine too," Betty Sue said.

"Oh, that's right, I already forgot, I—"

Betty Sue overrode her. "So, it'll be like both of us are taking our purses."

"Right," Karen said. She tilted her head back slowly, stuck her chin out, and smiled when she said the word.

They stepped out of the car onto the gravel lot. Small groups of people moved through the main gate adjacent to the concession stand and dance hall. An old man wearing a green mesh VFW cap and a green vest covered in ribbons and buttons was sitting comfortably in a folding metal chair at the gate. He slowly and deliberately tore each person's ticket. When we reached the old vet, Betty Sue smiled, laughed, and explained in a musical roundabout way for everyone within earshot that we were there as guests of BH Hill and didn't really *need* tickets at the gate. The old man seemed confused but waved us through.

Just past the crowded concession stand, tended by busy grandmothers and grandfathers, I stopped, and Betty Sue and Karen kept walking. A man about my height, but older and heavier, walked up and smiled, showing off two silver front teeth.

"Hey, Jake."

"Hey, Cecil."

A short, plump girl walked up beside Cecil and held his hand.

"This is my new girlfriend, Wendy," Cecil said. "Say hello, Wendy."

"Hello Wendy," she said and laughed at her joke.

"Jake and his big brother, Alton, used to cut cedar posts off of our ranch a long time ago," Cecil said. His voice still had that lazy, high-pitched feminine sound. "They used to bitch that I never paid 'em enough."

"You didn't," I said.

Another, taller man, wearing a much-too-big black cowboy hat, lumbered up. He and I shook hands.

"Kent."

"Jake."

Kent introduced a different, plump young girlfriend and asked me when I was going skiing with them again.

"I still haven't recovered from the last time."

Kent smiled. "Man, that was fun. What, I guess that was eight years ago? Damn. Honey"—he looked down at the girl at his side—"this is the Jake Stewart I told you about. He's married to Susan Hampton, or I guess it's Susan Stewart now."

"No, you got it right the first time. Susan kept her name."

"One of those Hollywood marriages," Cecil said.

"That skiing trip's a legend," Kent's girlfriend said. "I never stop hearing about it."

"Yeah," I said, a twang creeping into my voice, "I think we pissed off the whole state of Colorado."

"Fuck 'em," Kent said. "It was fun. When are you goin' with us again? We're goin' up to Vail this year."

"I haven't had time to do anything lately. I'm just working a lot."

"Jake's a big shot now who works on movies," Cecil explained to Wendy.

"Really?" Wendy said. She and the other girl asked me what movies I'd worked on and what I did.

"He worked on *The Cry of the Plain*," Cecil said.

"Right."

"When's it coming out?" Wendy asked.

"It's supposed to come out in the spring."

"Didn't they film that here in Texas?" Kent asked. "I mean, didn't a lot of Texas people work on it?"

"Yeah," I said. "It started here in Texas, but they filmed it in New Mexico. There were a bunch of Texans involved in it, but the money came from the Newburgh Group in New York. I think it was a joint deal with Nepal Productions, ABC, and—"

"All right, all right," Cecil interrupted. "Don't talk that big-money crap with us, Jake."

"Right, sorry."

"Speaking of big money," Kent said, "do you make any working on those things? Maybe I'll get a job."

"Yeah," I said, looking at Cecil. "It's good pay, but you have to travel a lot, live in hotels, and you usually spend a lot. If you can get hotel and per diem you can save some money."

Wendy put Cecil's arm around her waist. "Did you hang out with any stars?"

"No, I was just a set painter."

"Did you see any stars?" Kent asked.

"Yeah, it was hard not to. Susan got me into a lot of the parties."

"I guess it don't hurt to marry into the bigwigs," Cecil said.

"Well," I said, "it's keeping me out of the goddamn cedar post business."

Cecil smiled. "Don't get mad, Jake. You're always so sensitive."

Wendy slapped Cecil on the arm. "Quit being rude."

"You can be rude to old friends," Cecil said. "That's what they're for. You want a beer, Jake?"

"I was just going to go buy one."

"That beer sucks," Cecil said. "Where's the ice chest?"

Kent pointed to a red Igloo cooler at the base of a live oak. "Over by that tree."

"Wendy, go get Jake a beer."

"You go get it."

"Golly," Cecil said, grabbing the girl's waist, "you sure are feisty tonight. Are you gonna be this feisty later? I feel like nursin' tonight, Jake, breast-feedin'."

"Why don't you shut up?" Wendy said. "Jake, do you want a beer?"

"No thanks. I'm supposed to be buying one for everybody else right now. They're waiting for me—"

"Okay, okay, we get the hint," Cecil said, walking away. "We're gonna go down here. See you later, Jake. Keep making that good money. Give that sexy Susan a big kiss for me." He giggled, and Wendy slapped his back.

"Oh more, hit me again," Cecil said.

"He's crazy," Wendy said. "Nice to meet ya."

Kent and his girlfriend picked up the ice chest at the oak tree, holding beers in their free hands.

"Call us if you wanna go to Vail," Kent said.

"Okay, I will."

"Say hi to Susan for us."

"See y'all later."

I walked toward the concession stand until the two couples were out of sight, then doubled back down to some steps and a box facing the middle of the arena. Betty Sue and Karen sat near the silver railing, their heads close together.

"There's Jake," Karen said. "Where were you?"

"I ran into some people."

"There's a lot of those around," Betty Sue said. "Have you seen BH?'

"No."

"He's always late. What do you think, Jake, we were trying to decide."

"What?"

Betty Sue straightened her skirt. "Should I marry BH?"

"Did he ask you?"

Betty Sue laughed. "Well, no, not yet. But I'm sure he will."

"He'd be a fool not to," I said.

"Yes he would, but you know, I don't think he wants me as a part of his life. He's built this gigantic new house, and it only has one bedroom in it. It's definitely a giant bachelor's pad."

As she spoke, a fat man with curly black hair and a thin, attractive, young woman discreetly listened from their metal chairs, three feet away. The woman kept tossing her blonde hair over her shoulder. The man propped a sandal-clad foot on the railing.

"I just think he wants to be alone," Betty Sue said.

"Do you want to marry BH?" I asked.

Betty Sue smiled. "Probably not. I can't decide. But he could at least do me the courtesy of asking." She turned and looked up the steps. "They should be here. Denny's really nice. You'll like him. He was a champion bull rider for years. He was also in the Green Berets in Vietnam. He's very close to the governor."

"Really?" I said.

"Yes, and he was wounded in the war and had to go through rehabilitation for his left arm."

"Wow," Karen said. She moved her chair closer to mine. I turned to look at her, and Betty Sue grabbed my arm with both hands.

"Oh my God," she said. "There's Calvin. Hide me!" She put her head against my shoulder, trying to conceal herself. I searched the passing crowd for Calvin.

"Who's Calvin?" Karen asked.

"Yeah, who's Calvin?" I asked.

Betty Sue released me, the danger gone.

"Somebody I don't want to talk about. I'm really thirsty."

"I feel an errand coming on," I said.

The heavy man with curly black hair leaned over and touched Betty Sue's elbow.

"Would you like something to drink, Betty Sue? We've got an ice chest, if you want a beer."

"Thank you, Joseph, but I'll wait."

Joseph looked at Karen and me. "Would either of you like a beer?"

"No thank you," Karen said.

"I'll have one," I said.

Joseph opened his small ice chest and handed me a can.

"All we have is light."

"That's fine." I opened the can and took a swallow. "Thanks."

Betty Sue readjusted her skirt. "Joseph, this is my son-in-law, Jake Stewart, and you met Karen. Jake, this is Joseph, and—I'm sorry, what was your name?"

Joseph's date tossed her hair vigorously. "Cathy." She smiled.

"Joseph's just returned from Italy," Betty Sue said.

"Were you there on vacation?" I asked.

"No, I live there," Joseph said. "This is the vacation, isn't it?"

"Absolutely," Cathy said.

Betty Sue stood up. "Karen, let's go to the concession stand and see if they're here."

Karen jumped from her chair and knocked it over. She balanced herself with a hand on my shoulder. "Sorry. We'll be right back, Jake. Stay here."

"Okay".

I watched them walk up the steps, their heads close together again.

"Are you from around here?" Joseph asked. He and Cathy stared at me sincerely.

"Yes, I'm from Cypress."

Cathy sat up, interested. "Oh, you are?"

"Yeah, but I live in Austin now."

"You know," Joseph said, "I have a daughter at the University of Texas that I like to brag about. Do you mind?'

"Brag away."

"She's in a very good honors program, and although her major is subject to change, she's making straight As there."

"So what do you do, Jake?" Cathy asked.

"I'm a painter."

"I think Betty Sue mentioned that," Joseph said. "You and Susan worked on *The Cry of the Plain*."

"Right."

"Did Susan work on the set as well?"

"Actually, no. She was a production secretary and then an assistant to one of the producers, a young guy named Ian Watt."

"And what does that entail?" Cathy asked.

I had another drink of beer. "I'm not sure exactly. It seemed to be a lot of gift buying and having dinner with people."

Cathy and Joseph laughed lightly.

"I've heard it's difficult to work on a movie," Joseph said.

"I guess so. The hours are probably the worst thing, at least twelve a day, six days a week. She and I actually don't get to see each other much during a film. She's with production, and I'm in the art department or on set."

"Where is Susan?" Joseph asked. "Betty Sue has told me so much about her, I feel I know her already."

"She's in Mexico right now visiting a friend of hers who teaches art in San Miguel. A well-deserved vacation."

"A lot of Americans in San Miguel," Joseph said.

"Yeah, I've heard that."

"Are you working on something now?" Cathy asked.

"No, but I'm getting ready to fly up to Chicago the day after tomorrow for another show, a feature film. I just got back from Santa Fe, so I have two days off."

"My daughter wants to get a job in films," Joseph said. "She's talking about it, at least. She had a chance to be a production assistant on something in Dallas, but she would have had to leave school for a semester. I talked her out of it. I think there's plenty of time for something like that later."

"Oh yeah," I said. "She should definitely stay in school."

"She's extremely smart," Cathy said. "And very beautiful."

"She sounds like a great daughter. I'm sure you're very proud of her."

"Oh, she's not my daughter," Cathy said. "I'm Joseph's mistress."

I nodded and became interested in the riders in the arena with their large flags, preparing for the opening ceremony.

"You're not supposed to tell people that," Joseph said, and held Cathy's hand. They gave each other a kiss.

"I know," Cathy said. "I just like the way it sounds."

A cowgirl came barreling past on her horse and threw some dirt over the bottom railing at our feet. I stared at a brown clod on the cement next to Joseph's foot. The man's toenails were long, curved, and yellow. I glanced back up the steps.

The grand procession began, led by an old, lean cowboy in a white shirt and brown hat. Two old, heavy Shriners in cowboy hats and red vests followed close behind him. One held the American flag, the other hoisted the Lone Star proudly. Making the circle, the two men began a duel of the flags; when one was raised, the other would be held higher or waved more, until they were both waving and shaking the flags like a baton routine. The lead cowboy broke rank and rode his horse elegantly to the center of the arena and faced the grandstand. The flagmen and the rest of the procession, twenty cowboys and cowgirls, formed a line across the ground behind him. Everyone rose to their feet and hats came off throughout the audience. Karen and Betty Sue came back into the box laughing.

They were followed by two middle-aged men wearing expensive cowboy hats. I shook hands with the smaller of the two.

"Jake, good to see you, buddy."

"Hey, BH."

A slight coke grind was working in BH's jaw. "You wanna go out to the truck for a second?"

I smiled. "Maybe later, I think this thing's getting ready to start."

"You're right, you're right. Let's watch this rodeo. Hey, this is Denny Hit from Victoria."

Denny stepped up from behind BH and gave my hand a quick extrafirm shake.

"Nice to meet ya," I said.

Denny looked away, smoothed his neatly trimmed mustache, and said something to Karen. BH greeted Joseph by name. Denny removed his hat, and everyone in the box turned to face the arena for the national anthem. A young girl led from the grandstand. No one in the box really sang. Soon the song was over, and we sat back down.

I sat next to Joseph. Karen started to sit next to me but then decided to stand and lean on the railing. Betty Sue took the seat and left an empty chair for Karen on the outside of the row. Denny Hit and BH were forced to sit in two metal chairs behind us. I turned to talk to them and asked BH how he'd been doing while Denny seemed to stare intently at Karen's tan shoulders and back. BH talked about UT baseball and a new housing development he was planning in Cypress. Betty Sue turned to us and ended the conversation with the announcement that the bronc riding had begun. BH and I dutifully watched the short event. Karen sat down in her seat, and Denny leaned over and spoke for some time into Karen's ear while Karen nodded and smiled, said "Uh-huh," and watched the rodeo. She then shared a secret with Betty Sue.

The bronc riding was over. Two clowns ran out and did a routine where their pants fell down and they aimed shotguns at each other. A little dog with horns tied to his head emerged from a barrel. A four-year-old boy, dressed in black as a gunfighter, was led onto the field and shot the bad clown in the ass with blanks. The whole show was narrated by an old man in the grandstand wearing a white hat. He kept wiping his face with a red bandanna. I pointed to the emcee and said to Joseph, "That's my old trigonometry teacher, Mr. Olcovsky."

Joseph pretended to suppress a laugh. BH leaned over and offered Joseph and me a Pearl from his ice chest. A sheen of sweat covered his forehead. Joseph and I took the beers, and after a few pulls, I asked Joseph what he did in Italy.

Joseph hesitated for several seconds. I watched the clowns set up for the barrel races.

"I'm a finger pointer," Joseph said.

"Who do you point at?" I asked.

Joseph stared at the arena. "People who deserve it."

Betty Sue and Karen switched places. I turned, and Karen was less than a foot away. She bent over and said, "*God*, it's hot." Her vest fell forward revealing small breasts with small dark nipples. Her skin was brown and damp. She wiped her neck. "Jake," she said, and looked away.

"Yeah?"

"The reason I didn't have my panties on was because my nails were wet." She held out her hands, palms down. Her fingernails were bright red. "I would have asked you to help me if I'd known you longer."

"How much longer?"

"At least five more minutes." She closed her eyes and smiled.

"Okay, I'll have a beer," Betty Sue said loudly from behind Karen's back.

"I want one too," Karen said.

"My God, Karen!" Betty Sue said in mock horror. "I feel like I'm corrupting you."

"I don't care," Karen said, tossing her ponytail in defiance of health. "It's the Fourth of July."

"Well, shit—here," BH said. He pulled two cold, wet Pearls from the ice chest and handed them out.

Karen opened hers and took a drink. Betty Sue tried to open her bottle and failed. She sighed. "I'm so weak. Jake, could you open this for me?"

Denny Hit quickly removed the bottle from her hand. "Here, I'll get it, Betty Sue." He twisted the top off with a flourish and handed the bottle back.

"Thank you so much," Betty Sue said and had a sip of beer.

We watched the clowns position three barrels in a triangular pattern in the center of the arena. Five cowgirls lined up at the starting gate, and then, one after the other, they pushed their horses as fast as they could go around the barrels. The crowd cheered each rider except for one girl who knocked over every barrel. But then, following Mr. Olcovsky's advice from the grandstand, they gave her a big hand anyway. The event ended, and a group silence fell on BH's box. Betty Sue dispersed it by telling everyone how her mother had been a champion barrel racer in Dallas.

"She was Miss Dallas two years in a row. Her first husband, my father, was a terrible alcoholic and calf roper, in that order. He never did as well as she did at the Dallas rodeo. He was very handsome but a horrible man. One thing he never let her do was wear red, and of course all she *ever* wears now is red."

"What happened to him?" Joseph asked.

"He blew his brains out with a shotgun."

"That's terrible," Joseph said. "Did she remarry?"

Betty Sue smiled. "Oh God yes. Five times."

Mr. Olcovsky announced it was time for the calf scramble, an event, he explained, where six poor unsuspecting calves are let loose in the arena and set upon by a score of hungry seven- to twelve-year-olds. "God help those calves!" Mr. Olcovsky boomed. "Remember now, if the child can catch the calf, and, more importantly, if he or she can hang on to the thing, that calf will be his or hers, as the case may be. Looking at the contestants here tonight, I think we've got some strong competition for the boys."

"Her fifth just died, though," Betty Sue said to Joseph.

All the children were lining up across the width of the arena. They wore the same outfits: blue jeans and white T-shirts with paper numbers pinned onto them by helpful parents. The kids milled about, fingers in their mouths, hands resting on best friends' arms, all more concerned with the crowd watching them than the jittery calves being assembled in a chute at the far end. A young girl, maybe five or six, with blonde hair tied up in a pink ribbon and jeans tucked into tiny red boots, wandered out of the line. Her bottom lip out, she staggered over the dirt clods toward her mother. The woman leaned through the railing and scooped the crying girl up and over to safety.

"What happened?" Joseph asked.

"Well, Mother loves to square-dance, and George just couldn't keep up."

"What happened?" Cathy asked.

Betty Sue laughed. "I'm sorry. One Saturday a month ago she asked him to dance and, well. . . ."

"No," Joseph said.

"He said yes, did one twirl, and dropped dead right there on the floor."

"Goodness!" Karen said.

"She felt terrible about the whole thing, but she has a new boyfriend now. She's only seventy-four years old."

"Wonderful," Joseph said.

Mr. Olcovsky's voice filled the grounds: "And here we go!"

The calves ran scared, staying close to the edge of the wall while children frantically grabbed for their tails, ears, and legs. A strong twelve-year-old girl quickly tackled a calf in full run, sat on him, and put her knee in his neck until his tongue came out. Two tall boys fought over another. The rest scrambled, dived, missed, and hung on until all the calves were caught.

Joseph asked me what was next.

I looked at BH, and he said he thought bulldogging was next.

Denny Hit spoke up. "They canceled it tonight."

"No," Betty Sue said.

"Yep," he said. "There's not gonna be any calf ropin' tonight either. They changed it all to tomorrow night for some reason."

"Oh no," Betty Sue said, "that's—I love calf roping. That's one of my favorite events."

"Me too," Denny said.

I asked Denny if they were having slack time later.

Denny shook his head. "Hell, there ain't enough riders here tonight to justify it."

"That's a shame," Betty Sue said.

"What's left?" Joseph asked.

"I guess just the bull ridin'," Denny said. "An' they only got five bulls goin' tonight. An' they don't look like they're worth a shit. That's it then, for tonight."

"Well, hell," BH said to me. "This ain't much of a fuckin' rodeo, is it?"

"It isn't," I said.

We watched the first rider sitting down on the bull, trying to get his hand in just right, under the rope. The bull was called Dingo. The lean cowboy in the brown hat and still-clean white shirt was backing his horse up in the middle of the arena. Another cowboy in a pink shirt sitting atop a tall bay was there to help him. Mr. Olcovsky told the crowd that Dingo had gored someone in San Antonio last week. The rider, a young man from Mesquite, got his grip, nodded his head, and they let loose the gate. Dingo came roaring out and immediately began to spin. Just before the buzzer sounded, he stopped spinning and changed directions so quickly he left the rider suspended in midair. When he hit the ground, Dingo turned back and flipped the man into the fence. The two clowns were quickly between the hurt rider and the bull. Dingo chased one into a barrel. As the clown ducked down inside, the bull crashed into the barrel and knocked it over. The white-shirted cowboy and his helper tried to steer Dingo back into the pen. The big bull veered away at the last moment and ran around the edge of the entire arena before the cheering crowd. He ran past BH's box. A long stream of mucus hung from the bull's nose.

"Ha! Get out of here!" Denny called to the bull.

BH handed Karen another Pearl and said, "Did you see that snot?"

Karen laughed. "Yes, it was gross."

His tour over, Dingo ran unencouraged into the pen. The other four riders came and went with lackluster bulls. The last cowboy beat the buzzer but had trouble getting off his bull. As the lean cowboy rode up to help free the man's hand, the bull jabbed his horse with a sharp horn. The horse jumped away from the bull into the fence and threw the white-shirted cowboy headfirst into a steel pole. He crumpled down into a manure-and-mud puddle at its base. The helper got the rider off, guided the bull back into the pen, and quickly rode back to get the other cowboy up out of the mud. The lean cowboy staggered for a few seconds, then limped back toward the grandstand, waving to the crowd.

"And it looks like . . . he's . . . he's gonna be okay!" Mr. Olcovsky said. "We'd like to thank the King Feed Company, T & R Auto Supply, the First National Bank of Cypress, the Cypress Chamber of Congress, Local 337, and every one of you who came out here tonight. Remember, tomorrow night we got a lot of things happening, so we're starting at seven instead of eight."

Betty Sue stood up. "Are you coming inside for the dance, Joseph?"

"No, we're going back to Austin tonight."

"You don't want to go to the dance?" Cathy asked him.

"I don't know. Do you?"

"Not really."

"Well," Betty Sue said, "we're going."

People began to fold up lawn chairs, close ice chests, pick up seat cushions.

"What about Sixth Street?" BH said. "I thought we were going to Austin."

Betty Sue shook her head. "BH, if you want to go to Sixth Street, go right ahead."

BH shrugged. "No, that's okay. We'll go to the dance for a while"—he put his head down like a sorrowful little boy—"if we have to. . . ."

"No one's forcing you," Betty Sue said.

"I know, I know. I'm gonna go put this stuff up in the truck." He popped out of his chair and carried his ice chest up the stairs.

Denny helped Karen from her chair. As he led both women up the steps, he put his right arm around Karen's waist and draped his other arm over Betty Sue's shoulder.

"Oh, good-bye, Joseph," Betty Sue called back. "Bye, Cathy."

They said good-bye in unison. I shook Joseph's hand and said it was nice to meet them both and wished good luck to Joseph's daughter at UT. They wished me the same good luck in the movie business, and I left them alone in the box.

*   *   *

Several teenage girls blocked the entrance to the dance hall, debating whether or not to enter. I stood a little straighter, said, "Excuse me," and walked past the girls. Inside I kept my head down and moved through the fringe crowd surrounding the dance floor. Four young men sang cover songs from the stage. I leaned against a table covered with plastic cups.

Betty Sue and BH came twirling by on the dance floor. Betty Sue stared happily up at BH's face. He spun her around, and they moved smoothly among the other couples.

"Jake!"

Karen leaned over the table behind me, smiled, and held up a finger. She walked at first, and then skipped around to my side of the table.

"Where *were* you?"

"Where were *you*?"

"*I*"—she said, looking over my shoulder at Denny Hit— "was trapped. I'd ask you to dance with me, but I don't know how to two-step. Plus these shoes hurt."

She balanced herself with a hand on my thigh and took off her shoes.

"That's all right. I'd hate to think what these boots would do to your feet."

"I could just stand on your boots."

I stood up, and she smiled, stepped up on my boots in her bare feet, and put her arms around my neck. I held her by the waist and we stared at each other for several seconds.

"I guess we could just stand here," I said.

Karen smiled. "Or—"

"Well," Betty Sue said, suddenly beside us. "BH and Denny want to leave."

Karen let go of my neck and stepped off my boots. She touched Betty Sue's arm. "Why?"

"They want to go to Austin, to Sixth Street."

"Do you want to go?" Karen asked her.

"I don't know," Betty Sue said. "I can't decide."

I turned. BH raised a plastic beer cup in salute from across the room. Denny Hit stared, chewing on his bottom lip.

"What do you want to do, Jake?" Betty Sue asked.

"Yeah," Karen said.

I sat back down on the table and crossed my arms. "I think I'll head back to the house."

"Go back to Austin?" Betty Sue said.

"Well, I was going to—"

"Yes, stay at my house. You shouldn't drive back tonight."

"Y'all can go ahead and ride with them, and I'll drive your car home."

Betty Sue smiled cheerfully. "Okay, dear."

"You know," Karen said. "I don't think I really want to go to Austin. Maybe Jake and I can just go back home."

Betty Sue shook her head no. "If you're not going, I'm not going."

Karen smiled. "Great."

Betty Sue turned slowly, examining the room. "O-kay," she said, her voice drifting into the lost-little-girl register. "I guess I'll have to tell them. Y'all don't want to leave now, do you?"

"Oh no," Karen said, fanning herself, "it's just so hot and crowded in here. Aren't you hot?"

"Yes," I said.

"Maybe we should go outside and cool off," Karen said, pulling at her vest.

"Let's go," I said.

"Okay then," Betty Sue said, "let's leave now. I'll meet y'all outside."

She walked back to Denny and BH.

"Maybe I should say good-bye to Denny," Karen said.

"Okay, I'll see you at the car."

"Oh, forget it. Let's go."

We left the dance hall. Karen stopped to put her shoes on at the edge of the parking lot. She stared at me intensely, her brow furrowed.

"You're just coasting along, aren't you, Jake?" She made a sweeping motion with her hand, palm down, and stepped firmly into her shoe.

I started to walk ahead of her, looking down at the ground. "I guess so."

We stopped and leaned, side by side, on the Toyota.

"I think that's great," Karen said.

"Thanks."

"Look, there's Betty Sue."

Betty Sue, keys jangling, pretended to be too exhausted to walk. "Let's go home and sit on the porch."

"That sounds fun," Karen said.

"We can have a glass of wine and smoke more of that evil marijuana." She turned her key in the door, unlocking them all with a click.

I bent myself again into the tiny backseat. Karen sat up front with Betty Sue. They spoke quietly of BH and Denny Hit. I let my head fall back on the seat and looked out the window at the moving cedars.

"Were they mad?"

"I don't know."

Betty Sue looked for me in the darkness of the backseat through her rearview mirror.

"Frankly, I wasn't ready for an evening with those two. They're going to be up all night."

"Right," Karen said.

We drove back through Briarcreek, the headlights illuminating live oaks along the road. The neon bowling pin and dry cleaner's sign appeared in the darkness.

"There's supposed to be a meteor shower tonight," I said.

"No, that was last night," Betty Sue said.

"Oh."

"But maybe we'll see some tonight," she added.

"Some stragglers," Karen said.

We pulled into the Hampton drive and parked under the balcony. We slowly walked back up the steep front steps and went inside. Karen went into the master bedroom.

"We're going to change," Betty Sue said. "There's an open bottle of red wine inside the refrigerator. You can get that and three glasses, please, if you like, and I'll roll a joint."

"Okay."

"Meet ya on the porch."

She waved and walked into the bedroom. I found the wine and three matching glasses, walked through the den, opened a sliding glass door, and stepped onto the deck. I set the glasses and bottle on a white table surrounded by wicker-and-metal chairs and lounges. I walked to the far corner of the balcony where a floodlight shone brightly out across the yard. Susan was perched on the railing facing me, her shirt undone. She unbuttoned my shirt and ran her hands along my back. I held her, and the wind blew her long hair into our faces.

"I have to get home."

"Don't leave."

"I'm late. I have to go. My parents—"

"Let's go back inside."

"Okay."

"It's beautiful out here, isn't it?"

"It is."

"I love you."

"I love you."

"We need to keep this screen door shut," Betty Sue said. "Be careful over there. All those boards are rotten. I need to get BH to get José out here and fix this deck. Or maybe someone will buy the house before it falls down."

"Probably be easier to sell the house."

"Probably." She poured wine into her glass. "Thanks for bringing the wine out. Did you have fun tonight?"

"Yes I did. I'm really glad I came out."

I took my glass. Betty Sue filled hers, and we toasted each other.

"To you," I said.

Betty Sue smiled and sat down. "To me. Let's light this." She lit the joint, and we passed it back and forth.

"Karen's wonderful, isn't she?" she said, holding in smoke.

"Yes, she is."

"She's incredibly beautiful. Men constantly fall in love with her."

"Is there one in love with her now?"

"Yes there is. His name's Chandler, an architect. They live together. He's very handsome, though somewhat older."

"Hmmm."

"She has such a happy outlook on life. She's very centered."

"She is."

"I think it's because her parents died tragically young and she basically had to raise her younger brother and sister by herself. It must have forced her to see the good things, made her very strong. Her own child is fabulous."

I coughed. "She has children?"

"Well, just one. April, who is . . . at least twelve, I think. She is a darling little girl—or really, almost a teenager."

"How old is Karen?"

"How old do you think she is?"

"I thought she was around my age, twenty-five or twenty-six, max."

"She's thirty-four, ten years younger than me."

"That's a surprise."

"She's come out here for two weekends now to clean the house."

"Does she clean well?"

"She's very thorough." Betty Sue took a hit and put the roach in the ashtray. "Do you want any more of this?"

"No thanks."

Betty Sue checked the den for Karen and whispered, "She said something very strange today, though, that's made me wonder about her motives. I really hate to be suspicious, but I think she wants to move out here and live in my house for free while I stay at Martin's in Austin and work on the screenplay."

"Where's Martin?"

"It doesn't matter, he's out of town. I have a room there now, you know."

"Oh, that's right. So what makes you think this?"

"I don't know." She looked up at the sky, then quickly back at me. "What she said was that April really loved Cypress and that she couldn't *wait* to see my house again and that all April *ever* talks about is me, my house, and how fun it would be to live in Cypress."

"And?"

"Well, April's never *seen* my house. And I only met her one time, a long time ago at Melissa Montgomery's house for about one *minute*, certainly not long enough for the child to develop a fixation on me or my house."

"How do you know she wants to live here for free?"

"That's how she works. I mean, she's really Melissa and Brian Montgomery's cook. And she cleans for them and takes care of the kids when Brian's on the road on tour. They really love her and give her everything. They even make her car payments."

"I see."

She stared, measuring my response. "I don't know. She's very sweet."

"And here she comes."

Karen slid open the screen door and walked onto the porch. She was wearing a pink Mexican house dress, her hair was down, and she had on sandals. Her toenails were painted red.

"I'm sorry. I had to call about April," she said and poured herself a small glass of wine.

"How is she?" Betty Sue asked.

Karen sat down in a chaise lounge next to Betty Sue. "Oh, she's fine, wonderful, fantastic. Did I tell you she wants to take singing lessons? She sings like a bird, though, already."

"I guess she gets it from her mother," Betty Sue said.

Karen sipped her wine. "I guess."

I sat up. "Do you sing?"

"I used to," Karen said. "I used to sing a lot. My ex-husband, back in California, used to have this jam band that was pretty hot. I mean, they were popular down around Hermosa Beach. He played the drums and they didn't really have a lead singer. So I tried to convince them they needed a female lead singer, but they wouldn't let me join. I think I could've really helped them out." She stared up at the sky.

"Can she go to school Monday?" Betty Sue asked.

"Who?"

"April."

"Oh yes, she's fine." Karen looked at me. "I really hate for her to miss school. She loves her school."

"Really?"

"It's this special school, see," Karen said, and touched Betty Sue's knee. "Betty Sue's heard this so many times. It's called the Walnut School, and it was developed in Austria years ago by this old psychiatrist named Karl Fratzholz. What they concentrate on there is the spiritual side of education. If a child doesn't grow up with a balanced knowledge of his or her spirituality, then it's like she's missing something, something just as important as reading and writing, maybe more important. I think it's more important. For instance, my daughter, April, couldn't really read until she was nine, but through the Walnut School, she's been given this sense of confidence, she's been wrapped in this spiritual cloak"—she ran her hands along her arms—"that consists of a strong sense of her inner self, the goodness in herself that enables her to function much better than other children her age. Now she's reading and writing at the level of a sixteen-year-old."

I looked up at the stars. The cloudy edge of the Milky Way was visible. "That's great."

"It's like white light," Betty Sue said. "You can surround things with white or pink light, and all that remains is goodness. I know whenever I think of Dean and the divorce, I surround him in white light and he exists comfortably there on his own, responsible for his own happiness. You are only responsible for yourself." She drank a swallow of wine. "You cannot, no matter how hard you try, make someone else feel the way you want them to, all the time. You're not responsible for their happiness."

"Or their misery?" I said.

"All you can do is give them your love and warmth and be yourself, and then they have to deal with it. You should do that with your stomach problems, Jake. Surround your anxiety in white light," Betty Sue said. "You have to release all of that negative energy about your father. No one is more responsible for how you feel than yourself. That recliner over there has just as much of an influence on your outlook on life as anything else. You can only do it to yourself. You choose to grieve or be angry. I did with Dean for years until one day I wised up and made the decision to take advantage of this life I've been reincarnated into and be happy. Every day, consciously decide."

Karen swatted a mosquito on her leg. She lifted her skirt to examine the bite, and her pale upper thigh came into view. "That's what the Walnut School helps you with. You get in touch with the things in life that are truly important, and then you know how to make the right decisions when you have to."

"Right."

We leaned back in our chairs, staring up at the black sky.

"You know," Betty Sue began, her voice quiet and steady. "I've been told there's an energy vortex behind my house in the backyard."

I had a drink of wine. "By the swing set?"

"No, I don't know where it is exactly. It was so strange. I met this woman at the Harmonic Convergence Costume Party in Santa Fe. I had come as"—she looked at me defiantly—"one of my former selves, a princess from a planet of Pleiades. Well, it turned out that this woman, Nancy, was from the Pleiades system, too, *and* she was from Cypress."

"What a coincidence," I said.

"It was. And anyway—oh, y'all don't want to hear this."

"No, tell us."

"Yeah, tell us," Karen said.

"Okay. She said that right in front of the hill, the area between the Henshaws' house and mine—she knew the Henshaws—there is this incredible amount of energy that is a conduit to the other side of the world. *And* that my land was in the exact corresponding place as the Pyramids of Egypt."

"Wow," Karen said, "that's wild!"

"*I* thought so."

"Neat," I said, and looked back up at the sky.

"So, Jake," Karen said, "tell us about *The Cry of the Plain*."

"I don't remember too much of it. It was mostly just work all week and parties on the weekend—quite a few parties, actually."

"That sounds like fun."

"Yeah, I guess it was. I wouldn't have been able to go to any of them if Susan hadn't been so well connected."

"That must have been exciting for her to be the assistant to the producer."

"The work seems to suit her. She has a good memory and is so—"

"Beautiful," Karen supplied.

"Uh, yeah, everyone definitely seemed to love her. I was constantly being told by people how the movie couldn't have been made without her. The producer she worked for, Ian Watt, is young and new at this. I think his dad's some big shot at ABC, right?"

Betty Sue shrugged.

"He is, and anyway, just about everybody hated Ian's guts because he was such a cocky little penny-pincher. Susan was the only person that could get along with him, so she served as a sort of liaison between all the warring parties on the set and the production office. She made herself essential, which is what you have to do. And she was friendly, which doesn't hurt either."

"She sounds like a sweetheart," Karen said.

Betty Sue sat up. "Is that the phone? Did you hear the phone?"

There was a faint ring.

"Yep."

Betty Sue stood up and opened the sliding screen door. "BH and Denny said they might drop by. They're supposed to call."

"You know, I'm getting kind of tired," Karen said, and yawned to prove it.

"I'll tell them not to come over," Betty Sue said and shut the screen door.

Karen and I glanced at each other and looked away.

"So," Karen said.

"So." I stood up and walked to the railing.

"I bet you really miss Susan."

"I do."

"You must have a really strong marriage if you can be apart like this."

"We've known each other awhile."

"A lot of trust."

"Right."

I stared down at the driveway. Karen walked to the railing and stood by my side.

"It must be really neat that she works for the producer."

"He's just *one* of the producers, and I don't know how neat it is."

"What?"

"In a way it kind of pisses me off."

"Why?"

"I don't know. It's hard to explain. I feel like . . . she's getting ahead of me somehow. She's learning all of these . . . words. The money language. I don't know it. Ian Watt knows it."

"But you've got a pretty neat job, too."

"Yeah, right."

"What's wrong with it?"

"I just . . . I'd hate for this to be the end, you know? What I do."

Karen moved closer and leaned over the railing.

"Ow," she said, and looked at the white underside of her forearm.

"What's wrong?"

"Something scratched me." She ran her fingers over the old dry wood.

"I think some nails are—"

Her hand stopped on my arm. "Here it is," she said, and ran her finger over the nail. "So you don't want to be a painter?"

"No."

"Why?"

"I'm sick of hanging around painters."

She looked up at me and smiled. "I'm hanging around one."

"They're not all as exciting as me."

"Betty Sue told me that you were really an artist."

"She told you that?"

"Yep. Do you still draw?'

"Not really."

"I'd like to see something you've drawn."

"Thanks, Karen."

Betty Sue opened the screen door. "They're already in Austin."

Karen sat down in her recliner. "God, where do they get the energy?"

"I wonder," Betty Sue said. She sat down and then stood up quickly. "I'm just throwing this out: What do you think about going to bed? Could it be bedtime?"

Karen yawned. "It's nice and cool out here."

"We've got a lot to do tomorrow," Betty Sue said, moving toward the door.

"Not too much," Karen said. "The house is pretty clean."

"It is, but don't you have to go to Melissa's and then Martin's?"

"You're right, I forgot. How did I forget that?"

"I don't know," Betty Sue said and opened the screen door. "Jake, you can sleep in Susan's room."

"Okay."

"Or you can stay out here if you want. I just *have* to get some sleep. You can have that roach if you want."

"Thanks, Betty Sue."

She came to me, stood on her tiptoes, and gave me a light kiss on the cheek. "Good night, dear. I had a lot of fun tonight. Thanks for coming with us."

"Good night."

Karen waved. "'Night, Jake."

"Good night."

They walked inside. I turned, put in a dip of Copenhagen, and spat down onto the driveway, twenty feet below. The bright bowling pin stood like a sentinel across the road. The dry cleaner's sign shone steadily. A gray cat emerged from the darkness at the corner of the deck and hopped up on the railing in front of me. I held out my hand, and the cat pushed her face against my fingers, making precise turns and purring on the edge of the wood.

*   *   *

In the morning, I took a shower in Susan's old bathroom. It had now been taken over by Betty Sue. Beauty paraphernalia was scattered across the tile between the sinks: eyeliner and shadows, lipsticks, a variety of lotions, brown vitamin bottles, and a special perm brush I'd been warned not to use. Several black-and-white snapshots from crowded photo booths were tacked to the wall. Betty Sue and Susan and friends, pushing one another aside to be in the center.

A picture of myself sitting on the front porch petting an alert golden retriever. A postcard of Kandinsky. A picture of Matisse writing a letter behind an industrial-size bottle of Clinique body wash. The water in the shower smelled like sulfur. The longer I stayed in, the stronger the smell became. I brushed my teeth, shaved, dressed, and went into the kitchen.

Betty Sue was washing dishes. A paper bag, filled with clothes, sat by the front door.

"Mornin'."

"Good morning. Did you want some breakfast?"

"Are you having some?'

"No, I wasn't planning on it."

"I'm fine then."

She rinsed three red plastic glasses. "I put some things Susan left here by the door for you to take back to Austin. There's a shirt and cap of Dean's in there too, if you want them."

"I do, thanks."

She put a dish in a yellow rack. "Are you going to go back soon?"

"Yeah, in just a minute."

"I'm not trying to rush you. You can stay as long as you like. I'm going over to BH's house, and Karen's coming with me. Then we're going back to Austin."

"I thought she was going to clean here."

"She's almost finished."

Betty Sue turned off the faucet, dried her hands on a towel. "O-kay," she said and walked around the counter and we touched cheeks. "I'm going to put on my makeup. Thank you so much for coming with us, and listen, we're going to

Calhoun's tonight in Austin for dinner. Tommy Joe's playing there, and I love Tommy Joe."

"Really?"

"Oh, he's fantastic, you have to join us. You'll love him. Melissa Montgomery is coming, and Karen, and Roger Allen is going to play with Tommy Joe."

"Roger Allen?"

"He's a new songwriter in town. He's from Vermont. Melissa's his new manager."

"What happened to Brian?"

"She still manages him, too, but, you know, he's already *been* a huge success so—"

"Now it's Roger's turn."

"Let's hope so. Bye, dear. Don't forget your things. We'll be at Calhoun's at seven-thirty."

"Okay, I'll see you."

"Oh wait! I found this the other day." She bent over and looked through a large straw purse under the counter. "It's that sketch you did of Susan at the airport."

I took the paper from her hand. "Oh yeah."

"She looks kind of tired," Betty Sue said.

"Or bored."

"Well, you know how airports are."

"Right."

"Bye, please come tonight."

"Okay."

I folded the sketch and shoved it down inside the paper bag. The front door was open. I walked down the steps and rummaged through the bag for my new shirt and cap. Several tin cans hit the concrete under the balcony, rolling into view.

Karen was in the garage, in the same pink Mexican dress from the night before, bent over a broken bag of garbage.

She picked up an open can of corn. "Shit."

"What's wrong?"

"Oh, this bag broke, and I have to put this garbage in my van and take it to the dump."

"Here, I'll help."

"Thanks, Jake."

The torn bag smelled horrible, bad enough to make us both gag. Maggots crawled across a dangling Styrofoam package.

Karen's eyes were watering. "Oh God."

"How long has this stuff been in here?"

"I don't know. Let's get it in the van."

"You don't want to put this stuff in your van."

"I have to. We can set it on the other bags of garbage."

She opened the back door of her new van, and we gingerly set the broken bag of garbage inside. We'd been holding our breath and let it out simultaneously when we shut the door.

"Thanks. I've got to sweep this out, all this cat food and junk," she said, and pointed to the garage floor.

I picked up my paper bag. Karen grabbed a broom and began to sweep vigorously.

"Well," I said, "I guess I'll see you later."

"Are you coming to Calhoun's tonight?"

"Yeah, I probably will."

"Good, I know Betty Sue will like that."

"Right. Maybe I'll see you there."

She stared at the ground, sweeping. "Okay. Bye, Jake."

* * *

On the back porch of my house I found a dead blue jay. I kicked the bird off the porch, got the cat food from the house, and filled a pink bowl just outside the back door.

A cat appeared and began to eat.

The kitchen was full of dirty dishes and a foul odor permeated the room. I opened a few windows and the front door, letting in a warm breeze. I plugged in some red jalapeño-shaped twinkle lights hanging over a window. There were still Easter decorations on the coffee table: a partially eaten and melting chocolate bunny in a basket with blue, yellow, and pink stone eggs. An old poster titled "Dentists of Detroit" hung on one wall, on the opposite, a Klimt print tilted, barely held up by a tack, next to a print of a stained-glass window by Chagall, still encased in plastic, beside one of my own acrylic paintings— a large portrait of Leonid Brezhnev—next to a remnant of painted wallpaper Susan had put up, suspended by two nails.

I turned on the stereo and turned it back off. I punched on the TV set, turned to CNN, listened to one news cycle, and turned the volume down. I went to my bookshelves, looked at all the books, and then did the same with a line of albums stacked against a wall. The cat meowed at the front screen door. I let him inside, and he ran behind the couch and hid.

"You better run, Jack."

I went inside the bedroom and looked at the clock. It was almost noon. I picked up a roach off the dresser and set it back down. Two suitcases stood in the corner, packed and ready to go. Plane tickets were lying on the top of one, unlosable. I lay down on the bed and stared at the water stain on the ceiling.

The cat hopped up on the bed and began to knead my stomach with his front paws. I stirred, and he jumped off the bed, stretched, and tentatively stepped across the carpet.

"I've got to do something, Jack."

The cat was silent.

"What do you think? Is it crazy to talk to yourself?"

Again nothing.

"Fine. I'm going to take a bath."

I went into the bathroom, threw the stopper into the tub, and started the water. I found an old copy of *Vanity Fair* atop the toilet and put it on the bath mat. I stripped down, got in the tub, and read for a while. The cat came in and jumped up into the sink for a drink from the dripping faucet. I threw the magazine back on the floor and stared at a poster of a tall blue Hindu god hung on the wall. The man was standing between a blue river and a green tree full of fat peach-colored birds. Four cows lay at his feet. They seemed lazy and happy and wore head ornaments.

I got out of the tub, dried and dressed, and lay back down on the bed. The cat came in and looked at me. We stared at each other for several seconds.

"I have got to get out of this house."

I went out the back door and drove over to the Magnolia Café on Congress to have breakfast. I had the Economical: two eggs, scrambled with cheese, bacon, whole wheat toast, strawberry preserves, a half grapefruit, milk, orange juice, and three coffees. I left a big tip and tried to start up a conversation with my cute waitress. She was busy and would only fill my coffee cup and smile.

I checked my watch: one-fifteen. I bought a paper and drove down Riverside to an eight-screen theater. I went inside and watched two films, *The Untouchables* and *Adventures in Babysitting*, reading the paper in the break. After the second I left the building, my back hurting from the seats. A liquor store was next to the theater. I bought a cold six-pack and took it to my truck. I checked the ashtray for roaches, found a tiny one, and smoked it. I drank two beers, finished the paper, and went inside for another film. It was some horror movie. I sat in the back row and covered my eyes repeatedly. Then, by the glow-in-the-dark dials on my wristwatch, I saw it was six forty-five. I left the theater, went to my truck, and opened another beer.

*   *   *

Calhoun's was an old gas station on North Lamar converted into a restaurant, covered in quaint old signs advertising beer, soda, and gas. I pulled into the parking lot and saw Betty Sue getting out of her Toyota. A light rain started to fall. Betty Sue screamed, covered her hair with a magazine, and grabbed my arm. We ran inside, our boots slipping on the pavement.

"Oh, that was—my hair," Betty Sue said. "Karen's already got a table for us, she's supposed to."

In the middle of the crowded room, directly before the stage, Karen sat, her hair in a ponytail, her tan arms resting on the white table.

"*Perfect* table," Betty Sue said. She waved to a man behind the bar. "Hi, Lin. He's the owner."

"Yes, I've met Lin."

"Hi, Betty Sue," Karen said, smiling. "Hi, Jake." She hit the seat next to her and touched my arm. "Sit here."

"Okay."

"Where's Melissa?" Betty Sue asked.

"She'll be here in a minute. She had to get Brian off. He's going to San Francisco tonight for a concert."

"Oh yes, she told me that."

Lin came over and gave Betty Sue a kiss.

"This is Karen," Betty Sue said. "I think you've met."

"How could I forget?" Lin said. "Hello, Karen."

Karen smiled regally, her hands clasped in front of her.

"And this is my son-in-law, Jake Stewart."

We shook hands.

"I remember. You're a very lucky man, Jake."

"How's that?"

"For one, you're with the two prettiest women in the restaurant—"

Betty Sue gasped.

"I'm sorry," Lin corrected. "In Texas. And secondly, you're married to the finest young lady around. I've known Susan since she was knee-high to a grasshopper."

"Lin's an old friend," Betty Sue explained to Karen.

"I resent the use of the word 'old,' Betty Sue, but I'm honored to be in the friend category."

"You're so sweet," Betty Sue said.

Lin told us to enjoy our meal and returned to his spot behind the bar. Betty Sue repositioned her silverware and took a sip of water.

"Lin has a crush on me. He wants me to go out with him."

"Why don't you?" Karen asked.

Betty Sue shrugged. "I don't know. He reminds me of Ashley Wilkes."

I laughed.

"And I've always hated Ashley."

Karen pulled a yellow Tupperware pitcher from under the table, opened it, and filled an empty glass before her. She daintily took a sip.

I leaned forward. "What's that?"

"This is my dinner."

"Looks a little skimpy."

"I'm fasting. This is a special diet. You want a taste?"

"Sure."

I took a drink and made a face. "Boy, that's great."

Karen laughed. "It is. It's very purifying."

"What's in it?"

"It's purified water, through reverse osmosis, a touch of molasses, lemon, and a little cumin powder."

"Oh, okay, I know that stuff. My wife was on that diet the last time I saw her."

Karen frowned and wiped a water ring from the table. "Oh really?"

A man approached the table, crouched next to Betty Sue, and they said hello. While they spoke, a tall woman came bustling toward the table trying to hang on to two large purses, a binder, and some green folders. She wore a white dress and a wide-brimmed, floppy straw hat, and was very tan. She sat at the head of the table, looked at Betty Sue and said "Hi" quietly.

Betty Sue forgot about the man crouched next to her, leaned over the table, and smiled. "Hi, Melissa, I love your hat."

"Oh thanks."

The waitress arrived and Melissa ordered a margarita on the rocks. Betty Sue and I said we'd have the same. At the last second Karen ordered one too.

"*Karen*!" Melissa said.

"I can't help it, I'm sorry. There goes my fast."

"I can't believe it," Melissa said.

"She's full of surprises," Betty Sue said. "I think it's my fault. I'm corrupting her this weekend."

"No, it's Jake's fault," Karen said.

Melissa stared at me. "Hello, Jake."

"Hi."

"My son-in-law."

Melissa took off her hat. "Yes, I know. Where's that darling Susan?"

"She's on vacation in Mexico," I said.

"That sounds fun, I *guess*," Melissa said, moving her folders to the floor. "I'm sick of Mexico myself. I almost got *rabies* the last time I was there."

Betty Sue shuddered. "God, that was horrible."

The man who'd been speaking to Betty Sue said hello to Melissa from his position on the floor.

"I thought you were in Europe on tour," Melissa said.

The man nodded. "I'm leaving Monday."

"With?"

"Chet."

"Right, Chet. How's Felicité?"

The man smiled. He seemed stoned. "Huh?"

"Felicité? Your *wife*?"

"Oh, she's fine. She's coming too."

The waitress hurriedly dropped off four margaritas at our table.

"Great," Melissa said, and took a swig of her margarita. "God, what a trip."

Betty Sue fluttered her eyelids. "How was Maryland?"

Melissa made a noise of disgust. "I'm telling you, the music business is so full of sleazoids. I don't see how Brian ever made it before I started managing him. Everybody is trying to screw us." Her face hardened, lines firmly set around her mouth. "Betty Sue, you just wouldn't believe it."

"What? I heard something—"

"You know, it was a Democratic fund-raiser, but I mean, from the very beginning, Brian was supposed to get paid. Good causes are great and all, but we've got obligations."

"Many obligations," Betty Sue said, closing her eyes.

"Exactly, well, Weinstein, or whatever his name is, started pulling all this donation talk crap on me as soon as we got off our jet. He knew we were recording it too, something I'd already worked out equally with the other, uh—entertainers, I'll call them—and this little bastard starts telling us we can't record unless such and such percentage goes to this party and this party, which were all basically him."

"Who does he think he is?" Betty Sue asked.

Melissa took another drink of her margarita. Felicité's husband left the table. "He thinks he's King Shit of Maryland. Brian couldn't believe how tough I got with him, but you know, he's too passive. He just keeps getting used by the same people again and again. He's got to stand up for his rights."

Betty Sue sipped her drink and glanced around the room. "How tough did you get?"

Melissa finished her margarita and motioned for another one. "Very tough. I told him I'd pull everybody out of the thing that instant and he could shove every thousand-dollar plate straight up his ass."

Betty Sue laughed and asked what happened.

"He knew I wasn't kidding and that all I had to do was have Brian pull out and everyone else would follow."

"Good for you."

"So it worked. He became Mr. Shmooze then. He really pissed me off." She looked at me and made a karate chop on the table. "I told him I'd chop his *dick* off if he ever fucked with me again."

Betty Sue's mouth fell open. "Melissa—"

"I'm sorry, these people are impossible to deal with." She laughed. "Brian an' them couldn't believe me. They were calling me 'Swifty.'"

Melissa went through the details of the concert and what a success it turned out to be and how Brian was off to San Francisco now on their jet at Weinstein's request. I watched Karen. She sat very straight, perfect posture, her arms still folded on the table. She was nodding and seemed to be faking her interest in the story being told. She glanced at me a few times. When the story was over, the table fell silent. Karen looked to me and turned on her bright, white, and pure smile with ease. We stared at each other for several seconds.

"You must floss regularly," I said.

Karen and Betty Sue laughed.

"I do," Karen said.

"You can tell."

Karen sipped at her margarita, which was almost full. "Gosh, you know, I haven't eaten anything all day. I can already feel this drink affecting me. Will you watch out for me if I get smashed, Jake?"

"Yes, definitely."

"Watch out everybody," Melissa said, "the Queen of Clean is having a drink."

The waitress returned with Melissa's margarita and we ordered. Betty Sue had the vegetable plate. Melissa and I ordered chicken-fried steaks with mashed potatoes and corn bread. A tall, skinny man with a pointed nose and long hair took the stage. He was wearing a black vest.

"I just love Tommy Joe," Betty Sue said. "He always sings my favorite old songs."

"He has a new album coming out," Melissa said.

Betty Sue nodded, unconcerned, watching the stage. A short man with short brown hair, wearing another black vest and carrying a guitar, walked up to Melissa's side. He put his hand on Melissa's shoulder, and they quietly said an intimate hello to each other. He then gave everyone at the table a bland but good-natured smile.

"This is my new client, Roger Allen," Melissa said. "He's a Yankee, but don't tell anybody. We're working on that."

Betty Sue, Karen, and I stared at him expectantly and got the bland smile again and an "aw shucks" shrug. His eyes were bloodshot and watery.

Melissa touched his arm. "Are you going to sing? Are you ready?"

"Yeah," he said softly, "later. I'm just going to play a little backup for Tommy Joe."

"Roger's going to play at the Cowboy Café later tonight,"

Melissa announced. "And you should all come or you'll really miss out."

"I'm in," Betty Sue said, holding up her hand.

Karen asked if I was coming.

"Are you going to be there?"

Karen smiled and turned to Betty Sue. "Am I going to be there?"

"Yes," Betty Sue said. "I heard."

Karen's face turned red, and she examined her drink. "What's in this thing?"

"It's called tequila," Melissa said.

"Well," Roger said. "I've got to go. I hope I see you all at the café." He looked at Melissa.

"We'll be there."

Roger left, and the table was quiet.

Betty Sue raised her eyebrows. "Hmmm."

"Hmmm," I answered.

"Jake," Betty Sue began. "I was thinking of going out to the car before our food arrived. Would you like to join me?"

"I'd love to."

We stood up and pushed through the mass of well-dressed people at the front door. Outside the rain had stopped, and it was another hot humid evening. We went to the Toyota, and Betty Sue pulled a long, thick joint out of the ashtray.

"I think," she said, "your truck is more discreetly parked."

We went and sat in my truck and smoked half of the joint. We coughed and said little. I stared at a red stain on the end of the roach.

"I can taste your lipstick."

"I can't."

I handed it back. "You're immune to it."

"That must be it." She put the roach in the ashtray. "I feel much better."

"Me too. Let's go."

Just before reentering the restaurant, Betty Sue stopped, twirled, and asked for an outfit and general appearance rating. I gave her the highest marks.

The food had just arrived at the table. Melissa was cutting into her steak.

"I'm sorry, y'all, I couldn't wait."

"Don't apologize."

I started to eat my steak. Karen stared at me.

"Jake?"

"Yeah?"

"Are you stoned?'

I took a large bite of mashed potatoes and nodded. "Yep. Is it that obvious?'

"No, you've just got this big grin on your face that you didn't have a minute ago."

"It'll do that to you," Betty Sue said.

We began to eat seriously and listen to Tommy Joe. He sang a song about flying over Dallas, and Betty Sue swooned. His voice came straight out of his pointy nose. Karen reached the halfway point on her margarita and refilled the glass with her special bitter drink.

"This thing's really strong," she said. "I haven't eaten anything all day."

Betty Sue offered some of her vegetable platter. Karen hesitated, then popped one slice of cooked yellow squash into her mouth.

"I've already ruined the fast anyway. I'll start again tomorrow."

When the plates were as empty as they'd get, we eased back into our chairs, and the waitress cleared the table. Melissa and I ordered more margaritas. Felicité's husband now returned with Felicité. They sat at the far end of the table across from Melissa and politely gave their attention to the stage. The waitress brought the drinks. I wiped some salt from the rim of my glass and watched the table in front of ours. A pregnant earth-mother type braided her little girl's long red hair into one thick strand. An older man wearing slacks and a short-sleeve shirt, his chest pocket full of pens and folded paper, happily sang along with Tommy Joe. An old woman next to him, her hand on his arm, watched Tommy Joe intently. The little girl turned a rigid silver bracelet in her hands, then put it on top of her own head, slowly crowning herself queen. Karen's knee brushed, and then rested fully, against my leg under the table. For the rest of the set, then, we bumped knees steadily and didn't look at each other. Tommy Joe finished his last song. Roger made a beeline back to Melissa's table, and Felicité and her husband left. Roger bent down and whispered something to Melissa, who in turn spoke to Betty Sue, who summoned the waitress and gave her a credit card from her Guatemalan purse.

"We're going to go over to the Cowboy Café and listen to Roger now," Betty Sue said. "Did y'all want dessert?"

"No, I'm fine," Karen said.

I handed Betty Sue a twenty. She said thank-you and put the bill in her purse. Tommy Joe came to the table and gave Betty Sue a kiss. Felicité's husband returned without Felicité and did the same. Lin Calhoun appeared beside her, and Tommy Joe commented that the line formed behind him. Betty Sue's eyes and smile took on a new, glazed shine. She told Tommy Joe how much she loved his singing and that she would return the next weekend. Melissa and Roger left the restaurant. Betty Sue rose from her seat, and the three men followed her to the door. Karen grabbed her yellow Tupperware pitcher. The waitress stopped Betty Sue and had her sign for the meal. I lingered at the table for a second. Several customers eyed it hungrily from the door.

Outside I caught up with Betty Sue and told her I'd meet them at the café. Karen was already starting her van.

Betty Sue jingled her keys. "Okay, dear."

"Was this the man I've heard about?"

"Yes it was. What do you think?"

"Not sure yet."

"Me neither, but he's crazy about me."

"Who isn't?"

She opened the door of her car and slipped inside. "I don't know."

*   *   *

I parked a block away from campus, on the west side of Guadalupe, and walked. BMWs, Saabs, Porsches, and pickup trucks sped up and down the Drag. I passed a bookstore, a hamburger stand, the Varsity theater, and a coffee shop—my old hangout, Les Amis—still filled with intense poets drinking espresso at wrought-iron sidewalk tables. A woman smelling strongly of urine, with greasy hair and clothes thick with grime, approached me on the Drag and said it was her birthday. I gave her two dollars, wished her happy birthday, and crossed the street to campus.

A girl dressed in black with a fat pretty face sat at the entrance of the Cowboy Café.

"It's a three-dollar cover," she said.

I looked inside the club. There were twelve or fifteen tables, a bar with a mirror on the wall behind it, and the stage at the far end. Two couples sat at one table. The others were empty.

"You should go in," the girl said. "Roger Allen's playing tonight."

"Oh yeah? Is he any good?"

"He's all right, but he knows Brian Montgomery. Sometimes Brian will show up and jam with him."

"Say, did you see two very pretty, animated women come in here? One has light-brown hair up in a ponytail."

"No."

"Oh."

"Do you want to go in?"

"Uh, when's Roger coming on?"

"About ten-thirty."

"Hmmm."

Loud music began to play in a large open room next to the café.

"There's a pretty good band in the Union tonight."

"Yeah?" I pulled three crumpled dollars out of my pocket and handed them to the girl.

"Are you going inside?'

"Not just yet."

"I have to stamp your hand."

I gave her my hand, and she stamped a small green cactus on my wrist.

"Thanks."

"I'll look out for those animated women."

"You can't miss 'em," I said and walked to the men's room. When I came out, a slightly drunk young man with long blond hair stopped me at the door.

"Hey," the man said.

"Hey."

"Eakin's sophomore Philosophy."

"Oh, right."

"Excellent class, wasn't it?"

"It was. Ol' Eakin's pretty sharp."

"Did you hear what happened?"

"No."

"He died."

"No shit?'

"Yeah, he died of cancer last year."

"That sucks. I really liked him."

"You're Jake Stewart, right?"

"Right. You're Josh."

"So what are you doing now?"

"I'm in med school up at Baylor."

"That's tough to get into, isn't it?"

"What, med school or Baylor?"

"Baylor or both, I guess."

"Two of my uncles went there."

"Okay. What are you going to specialize in?"

"I'm leaning toward neurosurgery. I've got two more years to make up my mind, no pun intended."

"I always thought you wanted to be a writer. I never thought you'd go the doctor route."

"Me neither. So how's your painting going?"

"Pretty good. I just had a show at the Patrick Gallery and actually sold a few paintings. I'm moving to New York. If that no-talent weasel Julian Schnabel can do it, I can. I got a little teaching position at Columbia to fall back on, though."

"Great—well, good luck, Josh."

"Take it easy, man."

I walked back up to the girl in black.

"They went inside," she said.

"Thanks."

Betty Sue smiled gently from her chair.

"There you are," Karen said loudly. "We thought you'd gotten lost."

"I took the long way," I said, and sat down beside her.

"Roger should start shortly," Betty Sue said.

"How is he?' I asked.

Betty Sue shrugged. "I like him. Melissa's a brilliant manager. He'll probably go far."

"Do y'all want anything to drink?"

Betty Sue contemplated the bar. "I'm thinking of having some wine but . . . I started with margaritas . . . what do you think?"

"I'm going to stick with my first choice."

"Me too. On the rocks."

"I wonder if I should have one," Karen said.

"It's your decision," Betty Sue said.

"Maybe I can have some of you guys'."

"I don't like to share, but maybe Jake will."

Melissa entered the room, her straw hat in hand, and sat down next to Betty Sue.

"Well, I'm here, goddammit," she said, smiling.

I stood up. "Are you going to have a drink?"

"It's a bar, isn't it? Of course I'm having a drink."

"Margarita?"

"Yes, a margarita. Sorry, thank you, Jake. Here's some money."

"That's okay."

"Here."

I pretended not to hear, went to the bar, and bought three drinks. I carried them in a triangle back to the table, and the conversation faded quickly as I sat down.

"When are you leaving for Chicago?" Betty Sue asked.

"My plane leaves at eleven."

Melissa took a drink of her margarita. "What's in Chicago?"

I hesitated, and Betty Sue explained that I was going to go work on a movie.

"Really?" Melissa said and smiled. "In what capacity?"

"In the set-painter capacity."

"Oh well. What movie is it?"

"There isn't a definite title yet. It's a TriStar picture, a comedy-action-romance-adventure with a lot of car crashes and guns."

Melissa took a drink. "Sounds like a hit."

"Jake worked on *The Cry of the Plain*," Betty Sue said.

Melissa nodded. "I heard that was a lot of fun."

"It was."

Melissa took another drink and ice clicked on her teeth. "Does Susan still—oh yeah, that's right. Susan works for Ian Watt now."

"Where's Roger?" Betty Sue asked.

"He's in the back learning how to play the guitar."

We sipped our drinks quietly and watched the Cowboy Café fill up with everything but cowboys. As soon as Roger came out and took the stage, Betty Sue and Melissa began to talk loudly about the Cattlemen's Ball and some columnist who'd made a fool out of himself there. Roger was singing an earnest, honest song and the now-full house was enraptured. Melissa and Betty Sue talked at top volume and laughed. Karen leaned over the table listening to their every word.

A woman sitting at the table in front of them turned in her chair and asked Melissa and Betty Sue to be quiet. They didn't hear her and kept talking. The woman gave them a second and repeated her request, adding, "Some of us are here to listen to the music."

"Shut up and listen, then," Melissa said.

The woman quickly turned back around and did so. Melissa began a story about a community-service television spot that went awry. I finished my drink. Karen and I smiled wearily at each other. I started to say something to her, but she looked over my shoulder and yelled: "Frank!"

A tall muscular man with a mustache stopped at the table and said hello.

"I didn't think you were coming," Melissa said. "Did Walter go to sleep?"

"I just put him to bed. Zelina's still up, though. Your mom's with them." He sat down next to Melissa.

"Betty Sue, you know Frank, our caretaker-slash-foreman-slash-babysitter."

Betty Sue smiled. "We've met once before. Hello, Frank."

"Hi, Betty Sue, how are you?"

"I'm fine, how are you?"

"Real good." He leaned across the table, and we shook hands amiably, exchanging names.

"You know, Melissa," Frank said. "You forgot to add tennis instructor to the list. Hey, Karen."

Karen smiled at him sweetly, and I felt a surprising twinge of pain. "Hi, Frank."

"When are you going to play tennis with me?"

"Tomorrow, I promise."

"What's with all the tennis talk?" Betty Sue asked.

"Didn't I tell you?" Melissa said. "We put in two courts."

"That's wonderful," Betty Sue said. "But why two?"

"It's an even number. Problem is, I hate tennis."

"Now," Frank gently reproached. "Don't say that. Tennis is a wonderful sport. Right Jake? Come on, back me up on this."

I nodded seriously. "Great sport."

Frank smiled. "We can learn a lot from tennis."

"I love tennis, too," Karen said, "but I'm so horrible it's embarrassing. I was never good at sports, except for Hermosa Beach volleyball."

"Another good sport," Frank said, "if you're into sports."

"I've got to tell you something Zelina said last night," Karen said. She went around next to Frank and started to whisper close to his ear, placing both of her hands on his shoulders. Melissa and Betty Sue polished off two more drinks. I joined the rest of the crowd and listened to Roger sing a couple of medio-

cre songs. When the set was through, the noise level in the room
rose up to the volume of our table. Several people stopped Roger
as he made his way over to Melissa. He smiled and laughed at
their remarks. I looked over at Karen, and she left Frank suddenly and announced to anyone and no one that she wanted to
sit by her new friend, Jake Stewart, again. She came over, sipped
from my glass, which was full of melted ice, and told me how
wonderful things were at the Montgomery Ranch and that I
had to come out there sometime and that maybe I could come
out before I left town and play tennis with her and Frank and
the kids and if not then, maybe when I got back from Chicago.
I said I'd try to and thanks, and we gave our attention to Roger,
who stood behind Melissa, his guitar in hand.

"Well?" he asked.

"You were fabulous," Betty Sue said.

"Wonderful, darling," Melissa said.

Roger put his hand behind Frank's neck and said, "I won't
ask you."

Frank leaned his head back and looked up. "Please don't."

Betty Sue and I looked at each other, and she yawned and I
nodded in agreement.

"Well, y'all, I had a wonderful time," Betty Sue said, and
stood up.

"Are we leaving?" Karen asked.

"I'm sorry," Betty Sue said and slumped dramatically, "I'm
exhausted. You can stay if you like. Your car's here."

"No, I'm tired too."

I rose from my chair, stretched, and said good-bye to the
table in general. Betty Sue and Melissa pressed cheeks.

"Where are you staying tonight?" Melissa asked.

Betty Sue examined the open zipper on her purse. "I'm staying at Martin's."

"Is he out of town?"

"Yes." She zipped the purse. "He's down in San Miguel de Allende with Ian Watt, but I have a bed over there. I almost have my own room."

"God, what are they doing down there?"

"Learning Spanish. Bye now."

"Bye-bye."

Karen said she'd see them in the morning and waved. She and Betty Sue and I left the cafe. Walking down the hallway, Betty Sue and Karen spoke to each other in low tones, sharing secrets. I trailed a few feet behind them. I stared at the walls covered with advertisements of upcoming films at the Student Union theater, three-by-five cards asking for roommates, rides back home for summer, bikes for sale.

Outside the building, we stopped on the corner of Guadalupe and Twenty-Fourth Street.

"I had a wonderful time, Jake," Betty Sue said. "I'm glad you came."

"Thanks for inviting me. It was fun." I stared at Betty Sue and felt my face turning red and hot in the darkness. Karen was saying something.

". . . tomorrow?"

"What?"

"Why don't you let me make you a pie before you leave for Chicago?"

"Huh?"

Karen laughed. "I'm making pies early tomorrow morning. Pear and apple. I can give you one before you leave."

"Uh, no, that's okay. I'm leaving pretty early."

"You don't have to leave *that* early."

"I really do, but thanks."

"I thought your plane left at eleven?"

The Walk sign came on.

"Let's go, it's our turn," Betty Sue said. "Bye Jake, have a good trip."

"It does, but I have to run some errands."

Karen frowned. "Come on, Jake. Let me give you a pie." She started to follow Betty Sue into the middle of Guadalupe.

"No, really—"

"I can bring it to your house in the morning."

"Thanks, Karen, but I have a lot of errands in the morning and then packing and all—"

A car made a left turn and Betty Sue screamed, crossing the street hurriedly before it, her hands up in submission.

"Okay, suit yourself. Bye-bye." She waved and ran across the street. Betty Sue was holding her hand over her chest and breathing heavily under a flashing red Don't Walk sign. I watched them go, their shoulders touching, until they rounded the corner.

*   *   *

I opened the front door to the house, and the cat slipped between my feet. I sat down on the couch. The cat rubbed its back along the legs of the coffee table, purring loudly. I turned and saw Susan sitting beside me, a new magazine in her hands, turning the pages quickly with a snap, stopping at a perfume ad, rubbing the sample on her wrist and neck, seemingly oblivious to me watching her, then suddenly tilting her head, her neck exposed, asking me if I liked the scent. I stood up, walked quickly into the bedroom, and rifled through the contents of a top dresser drawer. I found an open letter atop a pile of socks with a Santa Fe return address and read it.

Dear Jake,

Bills, bills, bills. They came to $1895.00. I took the check you sent me and deposited it in my account. I know you're worried about spending all of your savings but I think we're paid off, so: rest easy. I'm going to Mexico for two weeks to stay with Tina. She's going to teach me (she's promised) how to paint. Then, it's back to the states, where I'm going to work, work, work, wherever it takes me. Soon I'll be Queen of the Movie World and hardly recognizable. I've decided to fly out from Albuquerque instead of Austin. Please don't work too hard in Chicago and don't be so hard on yourself. Enjoy your life.

Love,
Susan

P.S. I tried to get your Pulse card to work, but it was futile. Maybe the ATM machine was broken.

I read it out loud: "Enjoy your life." I went to a desk and began to go through the drawers. They were full of old unfinished letters, empty postcards, safety pins, purple stationery, and dried-up fluorescent markers. I searched under the bed and found her journal. I scanned the pages, reading accounts of gin games, backgammon, playing spades with friends, dull jobs, and time on the couch, stoned on weed in front of the TV.

"Enjoy your life."

My legs started to shake. I sat down on the bed, rubbed my eyes, and watched the clock. Finally I reached for the phone and dialed a number. A woman's breathy, lazy voice answered:

"Hello. . . . Martin's not here right now, so please leave a message . . ."

I waited for the beep. "Betty Sue. . . . Betty Sue? It's me, Jake. Are you asleep? I'm sorry, this is important. Hello? Betty—"

She picked up. "Yes, Jake."

"Hey. Were you asleep?"

"No, I just got into bed," she said calmly.

"I'm sorry but, uh . . . hey, do you know how I could maybe reach Susan down in San Miguel, down in Mexico?"

"No I don't."

"See, it's just . . . something's come up, and I really need to get ahold of her."

"No, I don't think she can be reached down there."

"Don't you have Tina's number? I mean, she lives in a house and everything, right?"

"Yes, she lives in a house, but she doesn't have a phone. There's only one phone nearby, and it's a pay phone."

"Betty Sue, it's really important that I get ahold of Susan."

"Why don't you write her a letter?"

"No, you don't understand. I need to get ahold of her right now. This instant. It's very important."

"Is there something wrong?"

I started to speak, and my voice broke. I stopped, took a deep breath. "I'm not sure. It's this letter, this note. Listen, Betty Sue—"

"Yes?"

"What the hell is Ian Watt doing in San Miguel de Allende?"

"I beg your pardon?"

"You heard me. What's he doing there? He's not down there learning Spanish. And Susan isn't learning how to paint. It's kinda scaring the hell outta me, ya know? I feel like somebody's hit me in the stomach with a hammer."

"I don't know what you're talking about, Jake."

"Come on, Betty Sue, don't do this to me. They're having an affair, aren't they? They're having—they've *been having*— an affair for months, only now they're consummating the son-of-a-bitch. I should've known it. I—I cannot believe I didn't see this."

"Jake, this is very personal."

"Please don't give me that 'personal' crap, okay? I've known you since I was a goddamn teenager."

"I'm sorry, but this is something you should take up with Susan. This is between you and her."

"Look, I just want to talk to her, all right? I've got to get ahold of her. What do I have to do, beg you?"

"Okay, Jake."

"Do you have the number of the pay phone?"

"Just relax. Tina has a service she checks periodically at her house in Fort Worth. All I can do is call it and leave a message that you want to talk to Susan."

"That's it!? That's all you can do?"

"That's all we can do. Please relax. Getting worked up with negative energy—"

"You know *we* were supposed to go down there? To San Miguel. We planned it. We were going to go down there and live for six months. Jesus *Christ*!"

"Please relax."

"I think I'll fly down there tonight and break every fucking bone in Ian Watt's body."

"I wouldn't do that. Let me leave a message for you."

"No *wonder* I lost her at *every* goddamn party. No wonder every time I turned around someone was shaking my stupid hand telling me what a *beautiful*, *wonderful* wife I had. Jesus Christ, Betty Sue, Ian sat at the goddamn table right in front of me and told her what beautiful eyes she had!"

"That doesn't mean—"

"No, no, you don't know *how* he said it, you didn't see it. *I* didn't see it."

"I really think you should just go to sleep right now and try to think of happy things."

" 'Happy things'? The *happy* things are down in Mexico right now *sweating* all over each other."

"You don't know any of this."

"*Really*? Why the fuck was it such a big secret that Ian Watt was down there? Huh? You think they're not going to bump into each other in San Miguel? I mean, it's a small town, ya know?"

"Jake, just relax. I'm going to get off the phone right now, and I promise you that I will call Tina's service and leave a message that says you want Susan to call you as soon as possible. Okay?"

"Right."

"Okay?"

"Yeah, sure."

"You're not going to do anything drastic, are you?"

"I don't know, what's 'drastic'?"

"You're not going to fly down there tonight, are you?"

"No, and I'm not going to slit my wrists either, in case you were wondering."

"Don't be dramatic, Jake."

"That's right, I forgot. You and Susan have the monopoly on drama."

"I'm getting off now, dear. Please relax and think positive thoughts."

"Wow. 'Positive thoughts.' . . . So, this is it, huh? It's over. This is it."

"Try to get some sleep."

"You know, I have to admit: Karen was a *very* smart move, an incredible distraction."

"I don't know what you're talking about."

"Yeah, right. Listen, I'm sorry I woke you up."

"You didn't. Have fun in Chicago."

"Okay."

"Good night, Jake."

"Good-bye, Betty Sue."

The dial tone came on. After a few seconds I hung up the phone. I turned on a small, black-and-white television set near the bed but then quickly turned it off, before a picture could materialize on the screen.

FINDING THE CURE FOR CANCER

There were supposed to be four of us, on a Sunday. We were going to roll a concrete floor in the back of a large warehouse in far East Austin with a clear, lacquer-based sealer. The floor was half as big as a football field. Twenty-foot concrete-block walls surrounded it on three sides, and there was a steel-girder-and-concrete ceiling. Only one side around the floor was open, with four roll-up doors over loading docks.

I rode over with a painter named David, who was chain-smoking in his little Chevette and making me sick with the smoke. Michael Jackson sang loudly from the radio, "The way you make me feel!" I asked David to maybe quit smoking so much, and he said, "Hey, roll down the window."

Another painter, whose name was Ray, brought the supplies over in his truck: empty metal buckets, roller set-ups, lacquer thinner, a few drop cloths, roller poles, and about ten metal five-gallon cans of sealer. We started unloading everything on one of the docks. Ray was dripping with sweat, and he gave us a little Bic pen-cap bump of crank for breakfast.

He kept wiping the sweat off his forehead and cleaning his glasses over and over.

"Man, I'm beadin' bad. Six-thirty in the morning an' I'm beadin'. I'm goin'."

"Fast," David said.

We had most of the heavy cans unloaded. We stopped to look out across the concrete field.

"Man, this is gonna suck," David said. "Why couldn't we do this yesterday?"

"They were doing something in here on Saturday," I said. "Isn't there supposed to be another guy here?'

"Who?" Ray said.

I pulled a joint out of my shirt pocket, lit it, and passed it to Ray. "Some old guy. Cole . . . colon . . ."

Ray laughed. "His name's Colon?"

"Collin?" David said. "Collin?"

"Yeah, that's it. Mike said we gotta finish this today, so he was giving us somebody else."

"Oh fuck," David said, "the Rummy." He took a hit off the joint, gave it back to me, and lit a cigarette.

"You know him?" Ray said.

"I had to work with him last week," David said. "He's totally fucking worthless. He talks the whole time an' doesn't do shit. An' he's a fuckin' rummy."

"I thought you had to be a sailor to be a rummy," Ray said.

"No," David said. "I think he was a boxer in England or somewhere. He's punch-drunk on top of everything else." He started laughing. "You should see him try to paint."

I looked at my watch: 7:05. "Well, he's late already."

"That asshole, Mike," David said. "We really needed some help today."

"We're gonna have to work now," Ray said.

"Shit."

We stood out there and finished the joint. The sun started coming up over the buildings.

I took a deep breath. There was an odor of rotting eggs and old burning meat in the air. "What's that smell?"

"There's a chicken factory over there," Ray said.

"Speaking of chicken . . ." David said.

"Here we go," Ray said.

"You won't believe this," David said.

"You're right," I said.

Ray pulled out a screwdriver. I grabbed a stiff-blade putty knife, and we started opening all the lids on the cans of sealer.

David puffed on his cigarette. "My sister-in-law let me fuck her in the ass last night."

"Goddamn, I'm sweating," Ray said. "I can barely hold this screwdriver."

"Your wife's sister lives with you?" I asked David.

"Yeah, she watches the kids. Crazy bitch. She an' my old lady got all cranked up and horny last night. I been giving them go-fast an' trying to fuck 'em both for days. I finally got her to eat Sally out—"

"That's incest," Ray said.

"—and she had her ass up in the air, so I just got up there and started fucking the shit out of her."

"Literally," I said.

Ray started laughing.

"I did," David said.

"Sure you did," Ray said.

Ray and I both stared at David.

"What?" David said.

"Nothing," I said.

"Come on, what?"

Ray shook his head.

"You don't believe me, do you?" David said.

Ray wiped the sweat off his forehead. "No, I was just thinking how much you look like Mr. Magoo."

"You really do," I said. "Your head's too big for your body or something. You look like a freak."

Ray pointed to David's large dirty tennis shoes. "Look at those giant feet on those short skinny legs. You're like a cartoon character."

"Hey," David said. He inhaled on his cigarette.

"What?" Ray said.

"Fuck you."

Ray pulled a lid off a bucket and made a face. "God, this stinks."

"Is that lacquer?" David said.

"Yeah," I said. "It's lacquer, and you better put out that goddamn cigarette."

"No shit," David said, and flicked the butt over the loading dock into the parking lot.

"Did Mike send any respirators with you?" I asked Ray.

"Uh, no."

"Why not?"

"I guess he thought we had some."

"Well that's fucking great."

"Man, we're gonna get wasted," Ray said. He poured some of the sealer off into an empty metal bucket.

David bent down to read the label on the can. "That's okay. It says here it just causes central nervous system damage, lung cancer, stomach cancer, brain cancer. . . ."

"Listen," Ray said. "Two stupid motherfuckers broke into my house yesterday."

"No shit?" I said.

"Yeah, an' they took my TV, the VCR, my stereo, an' about forty-five grams of peanut butter all done up in little brown jars."

"Oh shit," David said.

Ray cleaned his glasses. "I know. I was really pissed. Catherine could have been there. She just turned eight yesterday, an' we were at my wife's mom's for her birthday party. We come home an' everything's gone."

I started setting up the buckets. "That sucks."

"So I made one phone call to my Bandito friends."

"I see," David said. "It was their speed."

Ray nodded vigorously. "They had those two idiots"—he snapped his fingers—"like *that*. I mean, not one hour. Those guys didn't go five blocks before they hocked my TV and VCR." He started laughing. "Right around the corner. These guys, these Banditos, are total professionals. I really enjoy dealing with them, except for the violence. They tracked these guys down an' called me immediately."

"Little better than the cops," I said.

"Right. So they called me up an' they asked me to come down there, an' they've got these two stupid Mexicans—"

"I thought you were Mexican," I said.

"I'm half Mexican, half Japanese."

"That explains a lot," David said.

Ray took off his glasses and looked at me. "Can't you tell from my slanted eyes?"

"No, they're too bloodshot."

"Anyway, listen to this. So, they have these two guys an' they've already beaten the shit out of them. An' Victor, he's the guy I deal with, real nice guy, normally. He pulls me over an' he says, 'Ray, I want you to hit them.' An' you know me, I hate violence. The Road Runner cartoons make me nauseous. So I say, 'No, no, no, come on,' an' Victor like insists: 'I want you to hit these guys.'"

"What did you do?" David asked.

Ray cleaned his glasses. "I hit 'em. I hit 'em both, one time, in the face. All those guys just started laughing. Victor said, 'Jesus, man, get out of the way. I told you to *hit* him. Like this.' An' Victor, he's pretty big, an' he just gives this one Mexican— I think they were straight over from Mexico—just gives this guy a bone-crushing blow. Man, he just caved that guy's whole face in. I could hear the bones crunching. That other guy saw that, an' he just started crying. He knew what was coming. They pulled out the two-by-fours and crowbars then, an' I just said, 'Man, I'm leaving,' an' Victor's like, 'Come on, man, stay, watch.' I said, 'No way, I'm gone. Thanks, but I'm leaving.'"

Lee shook his head and wiped the sweat off his forehead. "I don't think those guys made it, man."

"Did you get your TV back?" I asked.

"Yeah, but they kind of fucked up my VCR at the pawnshop."

"The moral of that story," David said, "is don't steal speed from the Banditos."

"Or big bad Ray," I said.

Ray started cradling his right hand. "My hand still hurts. . . . "

"I hurt my wrist yesterday too," David said.

I looked at my watch again: 7:35. "Man, where *is* that motherfucker?"

"I really feel like I should have gone to church this morning," Ray said.

"It's too late," I said.

"You're gonna burn in hell," David said.

"That's not funny," Ray said, and looked at me. "So what did you do last night?"

David and I had four of the buckets set up now, three-quarters full of sealer, and a roller and grid in each one. I started attaching the poles.

"Hey," Ray said. "What did you do?"

"I was finding the cure for cancer."

"Somebody needs to do that," David said. "I'm really startin' to get worried."

"Seriously," Ray said. "What did you do last night?"

"Fuck, man, I don't know. I got drunk and passed out in front of the TV."

"I've done that before," David said.

"I bet you have," I said.

We saw an old dirty yellow VW van pull up just then and park. An old man stumbled out.

"Hey, there are old people here," Ray said. He pulled out a small brown bottle, filled with crank, and took a little hit.

We watched the old man make his way toward us. He was very short and thick. He wore glasses, dirty painter's whites, an English-looking cap on his giant ears. I noticed that he walked funny.

"Goddamn," I said. "He's bowlegged."

"Leave it to Mike to send us a bowlegged, punchy Irish drunk who can't paint," David said.

"I thought you said he was English," I said.

"What's the difference?"

"What's his name again?" Ray asked.

"Collin," David said. "He looks lost already."

Ray waved to the man. "Over here, idiot."

The old painter slowly walked up and stopped in front of us. He was smoking a cigarette. His eyes were squinty behind his thick glasses, and his face looked like a plate of pink mashed potatoes. He smelled bad, and his fly was open.

"We were wondering if you were coming," David said.

"Huh?" Collin said. His mouth was hanging open.

"Oh, I forgot to tell you," David said. "He's deaf, too."

"What's that?" Collin said.

David shook his head and flicked away his cigarette. "Jesus . . ."

"How are you doing?!" I said very loudly.

Ray started laughing.

Collin nodded. "Oh, oh, good, good. Good as can be expected. Gonna do some rollin' today? I gotta roller in the car."

"That's all right," David said and pointed to the buckets. "Mike gave us four new setups."

"Huh?" Collin said.

"We've already got you one!" David yelled.

Ray started laughing again.

"Oh, I'll use yours, then?" Collin asked.

"Yes!" Ray said, nodding up and down, very slowly. "Yes, we, have, one, for, you."

"You might want to lose that cigarette," I said.

"Put your cigarette out, Collin!" David yelled.

Ray started laughing and held his ears. "Hey, man, cut it out, you're killing me."

"You gotta talk to him like that," David said and laughed. "He really can't hear. Put it out!" David said and pointed to the cigarette in Collin's mouth.

"What for?" Collin said.

"You're gonna blow us all up!" Ray said.

Collin glanced over at the sealer in the buckets and shrugged. He flicked his cigarette back over the loading dock and walked over to a bucket. He made a noise of disgust. "This shit's lacquer. Bad stuff. . . . You boys see the fights last night?"

"Here we go," Ray said.

"No," David said.

"Huh?"

"No, goddammit!"

"Well, you shoulda watched 'em. They had a little Mexican boy, Sanchez. Very fast. Hard hitter for a little man. Reminded me of myself in other days. . . ."

David picked up his bucket. "I think I'm just gonna drink this stuff."

I picked up my bucket and roller. "All right, let's hit it."

All four of us walked to the far end of the concrete building and set down our buckets. We then went back and spaced out the other full buckets of sealer, with their lids loosely on, at intervals along the concrete where we thought we might run out of material. Collin kept mumbling about the fight while he carried his bucket.

We walked back to the far wall, fanned out, a man every fifteen feet or so, and began to roll. The big room immediately began to fill up with lacquer fumes rising from the floor. I could feel the fumes going down into my lungs and moving up to my brain. My eyes began to tear, and my nose started to run. I looked over at David and he shook his head. "Man, this is really bad. . . ."

"Sanchez reminded me of Billy Lee McGraw. Truly one of the toughest I ever faced."

"What the fuck is he talking about?" David said.

"I'm beadin', man," Ray said. "This stuff is killing me."

"Billy Lee was a body-blow man—"

"This guy is killing me," David said.

I got nauseous. I could feel the lacquer fumes on my skin. My arms and my face were hot. I asked Ray: "You feel this heat?"

He wiped his forehead. "I'm tellin' you, I'm beadin', an' it ain't the peanut butter." He looked at me seriously. "We gotta move fast, man," and glanced over at Collin.

We were rolling and walking backward in one quick line, but Collin was lagging behind. We were already twenty feet ahead of him.

"Hey, Collin," I said.

He had his head down and was still talking. " 'Course they didn't think I could do it—"

"Hey, Collin!" I yelled.

He turned around, squinting through his glasses.

"You need to speed it up, man! We gotta move in an even line and get this shit on quick!"

"What's that?"

"Hurry up!" Ray yelled.

"Right, okay," Collin said. "I'm comin'."

He sped up a little but was still lagging. I was the fastest painter there, so I switched places with David and started catching Collin's slack.

"I was just a boy then, really," Collin said. "Just a boy, but that was what you did."

"Hey, Collin!" I yelled. "Are you from Ireland or England?"

"God save the Queen!" Ray yelled.

"I'm not a fucking Brit," Collin said. "Irish. Always will be."

"Hey," I said, "did you know anybody in the IRA?"

"What's the IRA?" David asked.

"It's like the IRS," Ray said.

"God fuckin' bless 'em," Collin said. "Every one. Not like the movies, though, you know. Not like the papers say. We were all in the IRA in my town."

"Man, this shit is really starting to fuck me up," Ray said. "My arms are getting tired."

"Mine too," David said. He started to slow down a little.

"They said maybe, you know, little things. They'd say—well, my uncle did—'Collin, go bury these bags over there,' an' you know, it would have rifles in it, maybe. Or maybe a grenade or two. My brother an' me, I was just a boy, we put a grenade in their fuckin' jeep. 'Just put that there, Collin, an' run,' an' it blew those two bastards into a hunnerd fuckin' pieces. One of them was a British sergeant."

"What's he saying?" Ray said.

"He blew somebody up," David said.

Ray nodded. "Cool."

We kept on rolling, steadily, staring at the concrete floor, turning it dark with the sealer. Collin began to slow down again.

"You'd do anything to get a Brit, you know. Sometimes we just threw rocks to drive 'em out, an' they shot at us. They shot my cousin in the neck for throwin' a rock. Just boys, really, havin' some fun, baitin' 'em, all of us . . . ," Collin let out a long, loud fart and kept talking. "There was a green field with . . ."

David and Ray started laughing. The terrible smell coming from Collin cut through the lacquer.

"*Jesus!*" David said.

"Man," Ray said, "this guy has some sort of internal problem."

We kept rolling, and I began to feel dizzy. My ears were ringing, and my arms and back were getting tired. I could hear Collin talking in a tunnel next to me.

"His Royal Highness, His Majesty. We had some fights on that ship that make these young Mexicans look bad, an' I beat every one of 'em. Everybody on the ship."

"Were you in the navy or something?" I said.

He looked up. "Huh?"

"Navy!" I yelled.

"Six fuckin' years," he said forcefully. One of his plates slipped a little and almost fell out of his mouth.

"I told you he was a rummy," David said.

Collin pushed his teeth back in and looked down at the ground. "They dropped me in Palestine. I was boxin' at home, you know, doin' well for meself, then for His Majesty. Those fuckin' wogs, though . . . that one wog . . . what was . . . he was there for a little while, but the Jews killed him. Bad people, really. . . ."

"It must be nice to have special friends in your head to talk to," David said.

"Hung 'em all up. Damnedest thing I ever saw. We was with the Security Forces, in charge of the withdrawal, think that was forty-seven or forty-eight, sad really, just buggered 'em, all of 'em, an' ran away. . . . I was protectin' several little . . . just that one village first . . . in the spring maybe . . . they called 'em Arab incursions, but they was just the local boys, Palestinians, livin' there, when the Jews took over the hill next to 'em. An' they only killed one Jew. Just one fuckin' Jew, an' we went in with 'em that night an' we took all their guns, most of us left, but some of them stayed, an' the Jews were . . . I'm tellin' ya, I never seen nothin' like it the next mornin', you looked out across that little hill an' there weren't one tree, one pole, one buildin', that didn't have a fuckin' wog hangin' from it. Men, women, little boys, little girls, they hung every last person in that village. It made me sick, it did. For one fuckin' Jew."

"What's with those Jews?" David said.

"First they kill Jesus . . . ," I said.

"They're still pissed at the Nazis," Ray said.

"What's with those Nazis?" David said.

I noticed my roller pole move in my hands. It blurred and came back into focus.

"Hey, we need to take a break from these fumes," I said.

"I never really fought a Jew," Collin said. "I wanted to. I saw some fight, an' they were tough. Not like a wog. Never saw a wog fighter, not a boxer among 'em. . . ."

Ray put his roller in his bucket. "I'm stopping right here, man."

"All right," I said. "Let's take a break. Collin!"

"When the sun came up, they were shootin' those that were still movin'. . . ."

David put his roller in his bucket. "Just let him keep going. Maybe he'll finish it."

"Not today," I said. "Collin!"

"Huh?" He turned to look at me.

I made the motion of breaking a stick with both hands. "Break!"

Collin nodded his head rapidly. "There you go, let's break it then." He dropped his pole on the ground and immediately walked past us, limping along quickly. He hurried out of the building, across the loading docks, and practically ran to his van.

"I guess it's teatime," David said.

We stepped outside onto the loading docks, and all of us breathed deeply for a minute.

"*That* is dangerous in there," David said.

I pulled a thick joint out of my shirt pocket. "It is. We better smoke this joint quick."

"Did I tell you I like this guy?" Ray said.

We lit up and stood there smoking.

"I can't smell that chicken factory anymore," I said.

"I can't smell shit anymore," Ray said. He pulled out a vial and had a bump. "You want some more?"

I said no.

"I'll take some," David said, and Ray gave him a bump.

We stood there, passing the joint. David lit a cigarette. I looked up at the sky and it was blue.

"I went to one of those porno video places last week," David said.

"Here we go," Ray said.

"I wanted to rent a gang-bang flick for me an' the old lady to watch. I got this Hawaiian one starring Kim Iyawannalaya—"

"Right," I said.

"So we start watchin' it an' I'm finally getting a hard-on, an' this movie just starts gettin' disgustin'. You know, I like to see one woman with maybe two, three guys—four's a bit much—but this bitch is gettin' fucked by like a hundred guys. They had her up on two sticks or somethin', like a pig over a fire, so they could all get around and fill every orifice. After the first few guys, it was like an assembly line."

"You know, that's somebody's daughter," Ray said.

David puffed on his cigarette. "Actually she was more like somebody's mother. Either way, it was disgustin'. Sally got all pissed off an' wouldn't fuck me."

I took a hit on the joint and held my breath. "I watched that movie *The Fly* last night."

I passed Ray the joint, and he stared at me. "I thought you said you didn't do anything."

I let out the smoke slowly. "That's not doing anything."

"I've seen that movie about fifty times," David said. "My kids love it."

"Yeah, I'd never seen it."

Ray passed the joint to David. "What, you don't have cable or something?"

"No, I got it. I just never watched it."

"What did you think of it?" Ray asked. He and David looked at me.

"I don't know, I thought it was kind of stupid."

"I think it would be cool to be a fly," David said and handed me the joint.

"Yeah, so you could land on a pile of shit," I said.

Ray started laughing and said to me, "Seriously, I think it would be pretty heavy to turn into a fly."

I shrugged. "Whatever. We better get back in there."

Collin started wandering back over from his van. He was carrying a paper bag and swaying.

"I think I could handle it," David said.

"You've already got the dick for it," Ray said.

Collin stopped in front of us. "What are you boys talking about?"

"We're talking about fly dicks," Ray said.

Collin looked confused. "Floor wax?"

David started laughing. "Yeah, floor wax. What brand do you like?"

"I can't hear you," Collin said. He was holding the crumpled bag. He unscrewed the lid of the bottle inside and took a long pull.

"Doing it in broad daylight now?" Ray said.

"Huh?" Collin said.

"Having a drink, are we?!" Ray shouted.

"You want a drink?" Collin asked.

"Jesus," David said. "I feel like I'm in that 'Who's on First' routine."

"Who's on what?" Collin asked.

"See?" David said, laughing.

"I tell ya, boys, you shoulda seen that fight. Ol' Billy Lee McGraw could hit like no man I ever met. . . ." Collin took another pull. "But I could take any punch he gave."

"Did you ever take any to the head?" David asked him.

Ray and I started laughing.

"Why are you laughing? Listen, I can take a punch from any man. I've got an iron stomach," he said, and hit himself in the gut. "See, feel that."

"No thanks," I said.

"An iron stomach."

"Full of rum," David said.

"Hey, Collin," Ray said, "did you just hear a bell somewhere?"

"Huh?"

"I think the round's over," Ray said. "The fight's over."

"Yeah, and you lost," David said.

Ray and I started laughing again. The old man grew angry and started taking off his long-sleeve shirt. He had a dirty white tank top on, stretched over his flabby gut.

"Uh-oh," David said. "Maybe somebody has had too much to drink—"

"What the hell are you boys laughin' at, huh? Is it that dope you're smokin'? Well, let me tell you, I been takin' punches all my life, an' I can take one in the gut from any man. Even Billy Lee McGraw." The old man stepped back and crouched down a little, tightening his gut. "Who wants to try?" he said loudly.

"Somebody has *definitely* had too much to drink," David said, and lit another cigarette.

"Hey, Collin," I said, "I think we better get back to work, man."

"Goddammit!" Collin yelled. "You don't believe me, do you? Who wants to take a shot at me? I bet none of you punks can hit me in the stomach and make me blink. No man could."

"Isn't the goal to hit *them* in the stomach?" David asked.

Collin turned to him and stuck out his gut. "Huh? You wanna take a shot?"

"Uh, no, my hand hurts. I was arm wrestling my little girl last night—"

"And she won," I said.

David rubbed his right wrist. "It really does hurt. I think I'm getting wrist cancer."

"Years of masturbation," Ray said.

"How 'bout you?" Collin said to Ray and stuck out his gut.

"Goddamn, man, you're still on that?"

"Take your best shot!"

"Shit, could you say that a little louder?" David said. "My uncle in Cleveland couldn't hear you."

"I tell you what," Ray said. "How about I just kick you in the nuts? I bet Billy Boy McGraw never did that."

"Billy Lee," I said.

"Right."

"Come on," I said. "Let's go finish the floor."

"Yeah, let's get it over with," David said and put out his cigarette. "These things are gonna kill me."

We started to walk back in, and the old man reached out and stopped Ray from walking.

"Hold it right there," Collin said.

Ray pretended to be pissed. "Hey, motherfucker—"

David started laughing. "Kick his ass."

Collin looked past Ray and pointed at me. "You! Wait, wait. You, come on, right in the gut, give me your best shot. I can take it—"

"You need to get to work, Collin," I said. "We can play grab-ass later."

Collin reached up and tapped my chest with his short fat fingers. I felt my legs begin to shake. "You, let's go, big guy. You even look like Billy Lee McGraw. I want you to hit me in the stomach."

I started to walk off. "Ahh, fuck this—"

David stopped me. "Hey, look, maybe somebody should hit him in the stomach."

"You do it."

"My wrist . . ."

Ray looked at me. "Well?"

"Well, what?"

"My hand still hurts from yesterday."

"So?"

"So hit him," Ray said. "Maybe he'll shut the fuck up."

Collin crouched down, ready for the blow. "Hard as you can now, boy. Then we'll go to paintin'."

I looked at the old man and his stupid cap. "You really want me to hit you in the stomach?"

"Come on, you smart-ass bastards! I'll show every one of you!"

"Maybe I'll hit him after all," David said.

"Come on! Do it!"

"Okay, man. . . ." I pulled back and hit him in the stomach

pretty hard. He doubled over and threw up all over my arm and got some on my pants.

"Holy shit," I said and looked down at all the vomit on my pants.

David started laughing. "He didn't tell you he was gonna throw up on you."

Ray was laughing. "That's his secret weapon."

"I guess that's how he beat Billy Bob," David said.

"Billy Lee," Ray said.

"Look at this shit," I said.

I walked over to Ray's truck, grabbed a white rag out of the back, and started wiping off. Collin had fallen down on his knees and was still puking on the concrete, moaning and heaving.

"That's a great trick," David said. "Hey, are you all right, man?"

Collin fell over on the ground and looked like he was in pain.

"Jesus, this is terrible," Ray said. "What a mess. I think you killed him."

"Hey, he asked me to hit him," I said.

"He did," Ray said. "We're your witnesses."

Ray and David watched him rolling around, holding his gut. I walked over and looked down.

"It didn't look like you hit him that hard," David said.

"I didn't." I bent down and looked at Collin. His teeth had fallen out completely this time and were sitting on the pavement.

"Are those his teeth?" Ray said.

"Don't step on 'em," David said.

"Hey, Collin, are you gonna be all right?" I asked. "Are you okay?"

"He'll be all right," David said.

"Listen, we better get on that floor," Ray said. "We're missing a guy now—"

I stood up and looked at him. "No shit, Ray. . . ."

Ray started to laugh. "Hey, you're not gonna hit me now, are you? I'll call my friends. . . ."

I looked at David. "I'll get my five-year-old up here to kick your ass," he said.

"Look," I said, "if you guys aren't gonna help me—"

"All right," David said, "let's paint it. This sealer shit stinks, though. It's gonna give us cancer."

"What about the rummy?" Ray said.

We looked at the old man groaning on the concrete.

"Fuck him," David said.

"You know Houdini died like that," Ray said. "Somebody hit him in the stomach—"

"So now I'm a murderer—"

"Fuck him," Ray said.

We went back into the building then and started to paint. The fumes had gotten so strong, I had to tie several paint rags around my mouth and nose to keep going. Ray and David did the same, and we kept rolling, kept moving, as fast as we could. Everybody completely shut up, and we got into it and finished. We threw all the steel buckets into the back of Ray's truck. We didn't clean any of the rollers out. We tossed them into a Dumpster with the rags. The old man, Collin, was gone, but his van was still there.

"Man, I'm dizzy," David said. "That floor kicked my ass."

"Where's Collin?" Ray said.

"The liquor store," David said.

"He's probably in the van," I said. I pulled out what was left of the last joint and lit it. We took a few hits and stood there.

"Let's go see if he's okay," I said.

We walked over to the yellow VW van.

"Nice ride," Ray said.

We wiped the dirt off the back windows and looked inside. Collin was in there, curled up on his side on a little brown-stained mattress, passed out, surrounded by empty boxes, bottles, paper, and junk.

"I bet it smells great in there," David said.

"I think he's dead," Ray said.

"I think he lives in there," I said.

"Nice place," David said.

"Yeah," Ray said. "I like what he's done with it."

We watched him lying there for a second, his stomach moving slowly, in and out, with each breath.

"Shit, this is depressing," David said.

"You're looking at your future," I said.

"No," David said. "I'll be in a Chevette." He lit a cigarette. "I'm going home. You need a ride?"

"I'll give him a ride," Ray said.

I looked at him.

"You wanna ride with me?" Ray asked.

"Sure."

"All right," David said. "I'll see you guys tomorrow. Bright an' early."

"Yeah," I said.

"Later," Ray said.

We walked back from the van to Ray's truck. I started to get in and then looked up at the warehouse.

"I wonder if we should shut those doors."

"Why?" Ray said.

"I don't know."

"What are they gonna steal?"

"Nothing. I guess it needs to air out. They were open when I got here anyway."

We got in the truck. Ray started it up, and we took off. I found another little joint in my wallet and we lit it.

"So what are you doing tonight?" Ray said.

"I don't know. Nothing."

"Why don't you go with me to pick up my daughter? She's at my mom's house. We're all gonna go eat at Kentucky Fried Chicken."

"I don't think so, Ray—"

"Come on, man, come with us. Catherine really likes you. She thinks you're funny."

He was staring at me, waiting for an answer.

I looked out my window at all the buildings, the cars driving past.

"Sure. Why not."

I remember his daughter, Catherine, was a good kid, smart, and I didn't have anywhere else to go.

EPILOGUE

1989

I quit my job with Mike's Interiors and said so long to David and Ray. Mike's Interiors was deceptively titled as all we painted were the most toxic industrial jobs in the city, with no residential jobs in sight. I finally had enough one day when I got what the old timers called "a paint cold" even though I was wearing a respirator while painting a bunch of shitty pipes covered in asbestos insulation with warning signs all over them in some East Austin warehouse. I was using a poisonous oil-based stain killer with fumes so deadly and strong that they seeped through the shitty respirator Mike had finally issued me and soaked through my skin so that my nose started running uncontrollably with clear mucus, along with constant tears pouring out of my eyes until I became dizzy and started to pass out. I quit that day.

I got a job then painting dorm rooms for the Physical Plant at UT Austin, the same dorm rooms I had once lived in myself in 1981 in Jester, the largest dormitory on campus. Jester was so big that it had its own zip code, and we painters met in the bowels of the building along with Housekeeping, where we were mostly left alone. It was a humbling experience for me to have to wear my painter's whites and listen to some smart-ass freshman giving me shit while I and another painter repainted their dorm room. They would eye us with suspicion, as though we were criminals or rapists, and say things to me like, "Hey, make sure you don't get any paint on any of my shit, okay?" Or "You guys don't touch any of my stuff, all right? We know everything that's in this room, and we'll know if it's missing. Don't even move it." It was all I could do not to clock one of those little chickenshits, but I kept my head down and painted their walls. I needed the money.

I told my supervisor one day that I used to be a student there myself, in the very building we were painting. He was a nice old guy, and he mentioned that anybody who worked for the university who was a student could get a discount on taking classes. He also pointed out that I was the youngest painter in his shop, something that hadn't occurred to me, as I already felt like an old man on the UT campus at all of twenty-six. He suggested I go down to the registrar to check it out. So, I did.

I found out that not only would I get a discount on tuition but that if I would just fill out the financial aid forms—which were, yes, a pain in the ass—I qualified for all kinds of loans and even one grant because of my former good GPA and my several semesters of college. I applied for all of it then, every grant and loan, and got them all. I also enrolled in a heavy load of classes that began each afternoon and ran into the evenings, starting right away.

*   *   *

I was very busy then, between studying, reading, and writing, painting dorm rooms full-time, forty hours a week at UT, and then I would run into the locker room next to our shop and strip down from my dirty painter's whites and work boots and put on some jeans and desert boots and a shirt to run off to class. Some of the older painters gave me shit when I changed clothes like that, but they were okay; they were mostly laid-back retired old vets from years of American wars who had found a place to hide out the rest of their days in that deep basement paint shop, playing dominoes or drinking coffee and smoking dope just as much as they slowly painted the walls and hallways and stairwells and handrails of the dormitory itself. One of the first things they had told me, in fact, was to slow way the hell down when I started painting there, that I was knocking out too many complete dorm rooms a day just by myself, that they took things a lot easier there and that I needed to get with their program. So I painted and bullshitted with them during the mornings, and by midafternoon, even though I still smelled like paint thinner and oil-based fumes, I was at least dressed like a student and trying to stay awake in class. Now, though, I just wanted to get it all over with and finally knock out my degree as fast as I possibly could, to maybe try again and start over.

* * *

For some reason Susan and I still hadn't pulled the trigger on the paperwork for our divorce. She was working constantly also on any movie-of-the-week TV show that came into Austin, taking what she could get, still trying to move up the movie ladder. She was mostly landing short-term jobs as a production secretary, her goal then to work her way up to production coordinator to then one day become a unit production manager or even a line producer herself. She started coming by my apartment after I'd only been there a few weeks. One night she brought over her latest new boss, a friendly, middle-aged producer, an attractive woman with curly black hair. She and Susan were made up and ready to go out on the town in Austin and said they'd stopped by my apartment to see if I had any pot. I had a quarter-ounce bag in my desk that I hadn't been touching lately. I took it out and started to roll them both a couple of joints but couldn't find any papers, so I just said "Here, take it," and gave the older woman a full Baggie of good, sticky skunk weed. "Y'all have fun tonight," I said.

The producer and Susan, especially, thanked me. I could see she was still in her subservient worker-bee mode, the one you had to be in on any movie, doing whatever your boss wanted, including socializing off the set. Susan gave me a special knowing smile to drive it home and rolled her eyes, letting me know I'd helped her out in scoring this pot for her boss. But unfortunately this woman pulled out a couple of twenties and tried to give me some money. Susan tried to stop her but it was too late. She knew how insulted I would be and, worse, that I might say anything, and she panicked, ready to leave.

"Uh, hey, you can keep your money, lady," I said, irritated, and pushed the twenties back at her. "I was just doing you guys a favor."

The woman apologized, and Susan said a quick good-bye as I guided them both out the door and went back to work at my desk.

*   *   *

Susan started coming by more often after that night and we would have sex, still some of the best I'd had thus far in my life. I wanted to resist her, but it was impossible. One afternoon I was on the phone, and she came in my open apartment door and asked me to get off the phone, saying that she was in a hurry as she lay on my bed. I was talking to my mother—a rare conversation—trying to concentrate, when Susan slowly began to take off all her clothes and turned over on all fours and put her pale, round ass up into the air, moving it up and down as she looked over her shoulder at me and said, slowly, again, "Get off the phone." I hung up, we had sex, and then lay in bed for half an hour, holding each other and talking.

Susan grew quiet at one point and looked up at me. "What are we doing?" she asked.

"I don't know," I said. And really, I didn't. My brain was foggy, confused . . .

I wasn't complaining, but I got tired of her just coming over to have sex any time she felt like it and then suddenly leave. I wanted something more. I guess I was still in love with her. It got so obvious that she walked into my apartment one evening, as usual unannounced, no phone call, and she immediately dropped to her knees and started undoing the buttons on my jeans. It took every ounce of willpower I had to stop her. I grabbed her by the shoulders, pulled her to her feet, and said, "Hey, wait, come on. Let's talk," and she frowned, uninterested. Of course I gave in, and we got in bed and we did the usual, what we had done since we were sixteen years old, having sex slowly while we told each other everything, the complete truth, our innermost secrets, fantasies, and desires. I asked her who she was fucking now, and she told me in detail and asked me who I was fucking, and I told her of some prostitute I'd slept with only the night before, every sordid word, as Susan began to climax and we both came together, rested for maybe five minutes, and it was all over, as though we'd said and done nothing, and she dressed and left my apartment.

The next time she came over I was just too busy. I was sitting at my desk with five open books around me, typing up a ten-page term paper for my upper-division History of Modern China class, while she sat there at a cheap Formica table in my tiny kitchen on a folding chair, her legs crossed, bouncing a foot impatiently, smoking a Winston Light, watching me work. At one point I looked up and said, "I'm sorry, Susan. I really gotta get this paper done. The semester is almost over."

"No, it's okay," she said. "You're my hero."

"What?"

She smiled lightly. "You're the hero," she said and put out her cigarette vigorously into a plate on my table. "Going back to college, writing your *papers* and *books*."

I was too tired to care if she was being sarcastic. I just shrugged and kept typing. I sensed something lonely, though, left out, or lost in her but didn't have the time to talk about it, if she even wanted me to. She stood up then, gave me a peck on the cheek, and quietly slipped out the door, leaving it open behind her. The cream-colored stray cat, Sandy, was getting more aggressive, and I saw she'd bolted into the apartment just as Susan was leaving. I jumped up, quickly shooed her out, and shut the door behind them both.

*   *   *

I received the divorce papers a few days later. I knew we were split up, but I was still surprised. I shouldn't have been. I was the one who had moved out of our house in Travis Heights, who had suddenly quit working on movies with her. Even though we had both cheated on each other in our marriage, and even got off on talking about it, there was something different about the affair she had had with that line producer from England, that Ian Watt guy she had gone off to Mexico with for two weeks. It wasn't that she had fucked him—he was a skinny little uptight square, a corporate yes-man—no, it was the fact that she had lied to me about it so thoroughly. Or maybe just that I had been too stupid to notice it, that perhaps a genuine, however brief, love affair had sprung up between them under my nose, an affair that died, she promised me, the second she'd come back into Austin and found out I knew everything. But it was too late, I was too pissed, and I moved out.

Now, a year later, it was a midafternoon on a Thursday, and I was sitting at my desk staring at the divorce papers and calling her on the phone. She had given me the number of the production office of yet another terrible TV movie for CBS she was working on, this one directed by some C-list has-been actor for whom she was giving up five solid weeks of her life. I was still trying to read and grasp the details of the papers when I got Susan on the phone and she answered cheerfully with the name of the film.

"*Another Crazy Date Night!*"

"Susan?"

"Jake?"

"Yeah—"

"What's going on?" she said, adding quickly, "We're super-busy here. I got like three lines going."

"Listen, I just got these divorce papers you sent me."

"Right." She paused. "Wow, that was quick. I just mailed them yesterday. Or my mom's lawyer did."

"You're using Betty Sue's lawyer?"

"He's cheap. Hang on a sec." I could hear her answering another phone. "*Another Crazy Date Night* . . ." I was on hold then for a few seconds, and she came right back. "Sorry. This is the worst time of day, of the week. The Teamsters are bitching about the turnaround from yesterday, saying they didn't get a full eight hours or a second meal but—"

"Susan," I cut her off. "This paperwork . . . It just seems so . . . final."

"I know," she said. "It's depressing. I didn't even want to send it to you."

I sighed, torn but exasperated. "Really?"

"Yeah, really."

"Well, are you sure you want to do this?"

"I don't know. . . ."

"Do you want me to sign these papers?"

"I don't know Jake. Listen, hang on again—"

"Susan, don't put me on hold."

"I have to. Please just hang on one second."

I sat there as she got another call. I suppose another thirty seconds passed. Maybe one full minute. I could feel my ears turning red as I sat there and waited. I looked out my window over the city and realized that if I stood up and went out onto the balcony I could just see the building, the tall hotel she was working in, the production office right there, downtown. I felt like a fool, hung up the phone, and signed the last page of the contract.

I didn't even read the terms of the divorce, which was stupid. Her lawyer, someone, had put it in there that whatever each party had possession of in their residence at the time of the signing was their property now and forfeited to the other. I felt I didn't really own anything, but it hadn't occurred to me yet that—never mind the couch—by signing that document I would never get my albums back, my twenty-foot stack of records. I'd already asked Susan for them three times by then, and the last time she had said, "No, those albums are for your grandchildren," to which, well, I didn't know what to say or even what she meant.

I did see that I had to get my signature notarized to make it all final. I looked up a notary in the yellow pages, got in my truck right then, and drove up Lamar to North Austin to some cheap strip-mall office park. I went inside to a tiny office overflowing with papers and folders where an obese old man in a stretched yellow knit shirt and a lame comb-over took out his little silver round notary tool, crimped it down on the papers, and gave them back to me with a closed-mouth smile.

"Okay, there you go," he said. "You're divorced."

I must have looked a little down or confused, because he added, "I know. There's not much to it, is there?"

"No," I said. "I guess not."

* * *

I finished up the semester, took my finals. I had more than three weeks off from working on the dorm rooms. Our old supervisor at the UT paint shop was a good guy who gave us all a big break along with the students between semesters. He could easily, maybe wisely, have made us work the whole time over the Christmas break with no students in their rooms, but it wouldn't have fit with the steady, purposefully pleasantly slow pace they maintained in that shop in the mostly unknown and unseen depths of the Jester Dormitory, where we hid out and did as little work as possible, taking cigarette and joint breaks while playing games of washers beside the paint shop throughout the day. It was an easy gig, and between my loans and low pay it would just make the rent and get me through college.

A friend of mine from West Texas had told me about an old, mostly abandoned hot springs river and limestone pool with a couple of broken-down adobe cabins by it near the Mexican border, some cheap place in the middle of nowhere, south of Marfa toward Big Bend, about a ten-hour drive or so from Austin. He'd said if I ever wanted to truly get away from everyone and everything that was where I should go. He even drew me a map as it wasn't on any map, only an X off a caliche road in the desert near Presidio and the Mexican border town Ojinaga. I packed up my truck and drove down there, almost fell off a cliff driving through Mustang Canyon, but then found the hot springs, rented a cabin dirt cheap, and stayed for a month. There were only two people there, an old country couple who ran the place, which had a little grocery store and few visitors, only the cats and dogs the couple had, and the many surrounding coyotes, and a mountain lion or two, out in the hills at night. There was no TV, no radio, nothing but myself and the wind and the sky and the dry brown land.

I cleaned up. I got back in shape. I stopped drinking, quit smoking, no more crank or coke. I started running again, six miles, every morning, on a dirt road toward Mexico and back. I got all those poisons, all those paint fumes, all those toxins, out of my system. When I returned to civilization, to my apartment in Austin, it was as though I'd been gone for a year, to the other side of the world, rather than just a few weeks alone in the deep West Texas desert.

I had only one message on my answering machine when I walked in the door. It was from Susan. I punched the button. "Hey, babe, where are you? I came by and you were nowhere in sight. What are you doing? Are you out of town? Call me, okay? We need to talk."

I listened to the message one more time and erased it. I didn't call her back.

A couple of days later someone knocked on my door at two in the morning, in the middle of the night. I was in a deep sleep, and they really had to knock, banging on the door, until I woke up. I crawled out of bed, opened the front door, and saw Susan standing there in the amber porch light. She seemed shorter somehow, wore a black down coat, and had a worried look on her face.

"Hey," I said, and she just burst inside. I noticed, beneath her feet, the cream-colored cat running into my apartment right behind her.

"Wait, the cat. Sandy." I'd forgotten all about her. I felt kinda bad and immediately went to the kitchen, grabbed a bag of cat food, filled a little bowl on the floor for the cat and she started eating as though she were starving, and who knows, maybe she was. Susan had gone straight to my mattress and box springs on the floor in the corner. She sat down on my bed and leaned against the wall. I could just barely make out her full lips, frowning in the darkness. I was very tired and got right back in bed.

"I've been trying to get ahold of you," Susan said.

"Oh yeah?"

"Where were you?"

"What do you care?"

"Come on," she said softly. "I saw your truck here tonight. It's been gone for weeks."

Sandy came over and tried to jump up on the bed, but I kicked her off.

"Did you get a cat?"

"No. She just shows up sometimes."

"Where were you?"

"I went out to the desert for a while, down by Mexico, toward Big Bend. It's this old hot-springs place. It's pretty bare bones, but I liked it . . ." I could see she wasn't really listening.

"Yeah, look, I got this major job offer up in Nebraska and I really don't know what to do, if I should take it or not."

"Is that right . . ." I reached for a cigarette out of habit but suddenly realized, I'd truly quit. They were gone.

"I mean, it's a big feature film. But it's four months solid in Nebraska."

"So? That's good money."

"I know." She looked at me pensively. "Should I take it?"

"Hell, I don't know, Susan. That's what you wanted right? A big feature film?" I yawned. I was calm, relaxed. "You gonna be a production secretary on it or what?"

"Well, that's the thing," she said and paused. "I think so. It's just . . . you remember Ian Watt?"

"Uh, yeah."

"He's gonna be the producer on it."

I sat up in the bed. "You're going to go work with Ian Watt again?"

"I don't know, Jake. That's why I came over." She started biting her nails and talking rapidly. "This time he's an associate producer, not the line producer like he was on *The Cry of the Plain*. I'm not working *for* him or anything and, I mean, maybe you could work on it, too. I know they need a set painter and if—"

"Wait a second, wait a second." I shook my head, trying to wake up.

"What?"

"You came over here at two o' clock in the morning after you divorced me and we haven't seen each other in a month to ask me if you should go work in Bumfuck, Nebraska, with Ian Watt, the lying little prick who broke up our marriage?"

She gave me an exasperated sigh. "Give me a break. You know I didn't like that guy. This is serious, Jake, this is business. I'm just trying to ask you for the truth, for some honest advice on taking this show 'cuz it's a *long* film, this is a big commitment, and you're right, it's in *Nebraska* for Christ's sake, four months straight in the middle of winter. I'm not sure—"

She was working herself up again, and I stopped her cold.

"Hey, Susan?"

It must have been the tone of my voice. She seemed so nervous, unsure, and vulnerable there in the dark, leaning against the wall. We'd been together, off and on, for more than ten years, since we were sixteen.

"Yes?"

"I want you to listen to me very carefully, okay?"

"What do you mean?"

"Just listen."

"Okay. What?"

"I want you to get up out of my bed right now and get out of my apartment. And I don't give a shit if you go to Nebraska or Alaska, but I never, ever, want to see your face again. Do you understand me? Please just get out of here. Now."

Her long hair was hanging down over her face, and she didn't say a word. She pushed her hair back behind her ears, quickly stood up, and walked out of my apartment. As fast as she had come inside, she was gone and shut the door behind her. The whole thing seemed to have happened so quickly, it was like something I'd imagined. Like it never happened. But then I noticed that the cream-colored cat had indeed come inside my home and had somehow snuck up onto my bed. She'd curled around my legs and was purring now, burrowing herself into the folds of the blankets, weighing her body down deep, for good. So I rubbed her head, and I let her sleep. All she was looking for was a little warmth and comfort and a place to stay for the night.

ACKNOWLEDGMENTS

I'd like to thank Lora Fountain in Paris and Judy Hansen in New York for all their help in publishing my books. I'd also like to thank everyone at Liveright and W. W. Norton: Robert Weill, my editors Will Menacker and Phil Marino, Bill Rusin, and Gina Iaquinta. Special thanks to UT Austin Professor Emeritus of English Dr. Flowers for her wisdom over 35 years. And thanks again to Robert Crumb for all his personal and professional support for the past 20 years, helping me believe in myself and my work. Most of all, my deep appreciation to Carisa Valentine for her unwavering love and patient ear, listening to the struggles of a worrying writer. Finally, I want to acknowledge my father for making me a hard worker, which has served me well to this day.